home-grown
harvest

home-grown
harvest

delicious ways to enjoy your
seasonal fruit and vegetables

RYLAND
PETERS
& SMALL
LONDON NEW YORK

Senior Designer Iona Hoyle
Editor Rebecca Woods
Picture Research Emily Westlake
Head of production Patricia Harrington
Art Director Leslie Harrington
Publishing Director Alison Starling

Indexer Sandra Shotter

First published in 2011
by Ryland Peters & Small
20–21 Jockey's Fields
London WC1R 4BW

www.rylandpeters.com

10 9 8 7 6 5 4 3 2 1

Text © Ghillie Başan, Fiona Beckett, Celia Brooks
Brown, Maxine Clark, Ross Dobson, Tonia George,
Brian Glover, Amanda Grant, Annie Nichols, Jane
Noraika, Louise Pickford, Isidora Popovic, Sarah
Randell, Annie Rigg, Jennie Shapter, Fiona Smith,
Sonia Stevenson, Linda Tubby, Sunil Vijayakar,
Fran Warde, Laura Washburn, Lindy Wildsmith
and Ryland Peters & Small 2011

Design and commissioned photographs
© Ryland Peters & Small 2011

ISBN 978 1 84975 148 3

A catalogue record for this book is available from
the British Library.

Printed in China

Notes

• All spoon measurements are level unless otherwise specified.

• Eggs are medium unless otherwise specified. Uncooked or partly cooked eggs should not be served to the very young, the very old, those with compromised immune systems, or to pregnant women.

• Weights and measurements have been rounded up or down slightly to make measuring easier.

• When a recipe calls for the grated zest of a citrus fruit, buy unwaxed fruit and wash well before using. If you can only find treated fruit, scrub well in warm soapy water before using.

• Ovens should be preheated to the specified temperature. If using a fan-assisted oven, cooking times should be reduced according to the manufacturer's instructions.

• To sterilize preserving jars, wash them in hot, soapy water and rinse in boiling water. Place in a large saucepan and cover with hot water. With the saucepan lid on, bring the water to the boil and continue boiling for 15 minutes. Turn off the heat and leave the jars in the hot water until just before they are to be filled. Invert the jars onto a clean dish towel to dry. Sterilize the lids for 5 minutes, by boiling or according to the manufacturer's instructions. Jars should be filled and sealed while they are still hot.

contents

introduction

Growing your own fruit and vegetables is immensely satisfying – and is quickly becoming fashionable again. Food-loving gardeners are once more beginning to incorporate edible varieties of plants, as well as beautiful ornamental ones, into gardens that resemble the more functional spaces of our childhoods. Even in inner cities, where space is at a premium, many urbanites are finding that allotting precious space on a roof terrace or small patio for a few tomato or strawberry pots not only brings the benefit of the produce itself, but also provides a pastoral escape from a stressful lifestyle. And for those who struggle horticulturally, there is healthy growth in farmers' markets, especially within cities, providing local venues to buy the freshest produce direct from source and talk to the growers themselves about the best ways to prepare those sweet young carrots or deliciously earthy new potatoes.

This rise in popularity of home- or locally-grown fresh produce marks a deeply positive change in attitudes towards food, and is indicative of a quiet but growing backlash against a global, profit-driven food trade that lacks respect for the environment and the seasons and delivers disappointing produce. Food that travels long distances can be tasteless – harvested long before it is ready and shipped in refrigerated transport that stops ripening in it's tracks. Tomatoes bought in winter can be tough, floury and bland, nothing like the deep red, sweet smelling tomatoes that are picked off the vine in the height of summer. Additionally, many of the nutrients present when produce is first picked are lost during the long journey between the field and the plate.

In contrast, home-grown produce is cultivated with care for the environment – and you can taste the difference. There is great pleasure to be gained from eating what is seasonally available – paying greater respect to the natural order of the seasons yields wonderful results in the finished dish. Not only this, but putting in time in the garden can also lead to a healthy reduction in supermarket expenditure

But to say this to you, the holder of this book, is likely to be preaching to the converted. Your allotment, vegetable patch or even window box may already be abundant with fresh fruit and vegetables, but the dilemma is what now to do with this produce that you have spent time and care nurturing? One of the downsides of growing your own can be the sense of dé jà vu that haunts meal times. Dinners can seem suspiciously similar when all created from the same crop, and finding new inspiration can be tricky. For the home-grower it becomes customary for each visiting friend or relative to leave the house with a goodie bag laden with fresh fruit or vegetables that have become tiresome or that there is simply no chance of consuming before they spoil.

This is where **Home-grown Harvest** can help. Providing recipes for all your favourite fruit and vegetables, it ensures that there are numerous options for using each so that you don't have to cook the same dish time and time again in order to use up your produce. And because most seasonal locally-grown vegetables can be picked at their very best, many of the recipes are rustic and unfussy and truly let the flavour of the produce speak for itself.

The book is arranged as an easy reference guide with the recipes for each vegetable or fruit grouped together. Although, as much of the produce may be featured not only in it's own chapter but also in combinations with other fruit or vegetables, don't forget to check the index for other recipes, too. And be sure to take note of the handy tips, which offer further advice on preparing, storing and truly savouring the the rewards of your labour.

root vegetables

mashed potato pie with bacon, leeks & cheese

potato & parsnip croquettes 🌿 **indian potato curry with toor dhal** 🌿 potato tortilla with red pepper tapenade

roasted new potatoes 🌿 bay-roasted hasselbacks

potatoes dauphinoise 🌿 hash browns

sweet potato & coconut soup with thai pesto

sesame sweet potato with peanut dipping sauce

roasted sweet potato & macadamia nut salad

tagine of sweet potato, shallots & carrots 🌿 **roast sweet potato & chicken pie** 🌿 spiced carrot soup

roasted carrots with barley risotto 🌿 madeira-glazed roast carrots 🌿 **spiced carrot dip** 🌿 carrots with cream & herbs 🌿 **vichy carrots with fresh ginger**

carrot & walnut cake with cream cheese filling

parsnip, chorizo & chestnut soup 🌿 parsnip, apple & thyme soup 🌿 **honey-roast parsnip, carrot & shallot tart** 🌿 beetroot & beef tagine with oranges

cardinal's salad 🌿 beetroot, fennel & apple chutney

beetroot & horseradish relish 🌿 mini chocolate, beetroot & cherry cakes

If you've got a successful crop of potatoes this year and you need inspiration for how best to use them, this pie is a great option. Bacon, leeks and cheese make a particularly perfect trio, but you can add just about anything to this versatile dish. You should have potatoes at the very least, and cheese of some sort, and something green for a bit of colour – after that, anything goes! The croquettes are particularly good if you grow a floury variety of potato as it fluffs up nicely when boiled and mashed. The parsnip adds an interesting flavour dimension, as it is a little bitter and sweet at the same time.

mashed potato pie with bacon, leeks & cheese

1 kg floury potatoes, peeled

2 tablespoons olive oil

1 onion, finely chopped

2 small leeks, thinly sliced

90 g bacon or pancetta, diced

30 g butter

250 ml milk or single cream (or a bit of both)

1 egg, beaten

a pinch of paprika

a large handful of fresh parsley leaves, chopped

90 g firm cheese, such as Gruyère, grated

sea salt and freshly ground black pepper

a 24-cm round baking dish, well buttered

serves 4–6

Halve or quarter the potatoes depending on their size; they should be about the same to cook evenly. Put them in a large saucepan, add sufficient cold water to cover, salt well and bring to the boil. Simmer for about 20 minutes, until tender.

Meanwhile, heat the oil in a frying pan set over low heat. Add the onion and leeks and cook gently for about 10 minutes, until soft. Add the bacon and cook for 3–5 minutes, until just browned. Season with salt and set aside.

Preheat the oven to 190°C (375°F) Gas 5. Drain the potatoes and mash coarsely, mixing in the butter and milk. Season well and add the egg. Stir to combine thoroughly.

Stir in the leek mixture, paprika, parsley and half the cheese. Transfer to the prepared baking dish and spread evenly. Sprinkle over the remaining cheese and bake in the preheated oven for 35–45 minutes, until well browned. Serve immediately.

potato & parsnip croquettes

500 g potatoes, peeled and quartered

1 parsnip, peeled and quartered

25 g butter, plus 1 tablespoon for frying

2 tablespoons finely chopped fresh parsley

2 eggs

100 g dry breadcrumbs from a day-old loaf of bread

2 tablespoons plain flour, for dusting

vegetable oil, for shallow-frying

sea salt and freshly ground black pepper

sweet German mustard, to serve

makes 18 croquettes

Put the potatoes and parsnip in a large saucepan and cover with boiling water. Set over high heat and boil for 12–15 minutes until tender. Drain and return to the warm pan. Add the 25 g butter and mash well until the mixture is lump-free. Stir in the parsley and season well with salt and pepper. Cover and refrigerate until the mixture is completely chilled.

Break the eggs into a bowl and beat well to combine. Put the breadcrumbs in a separate bowl. Lightly flour your hands and work surface. Take 1 heaped tablespoon of the potato mixture and form it into a small sausage, tapping the ends on the floured work surface so that they are flattened rather than tapered. Dip the croquette in the beaten egg, then roll it in the crumbs until coated. Put on a baking tray lined with baking paper. Repeat until all of the potato mixture has been used and refrigerate until ready to cook.

Put the 1 tablespoon butter in a frying pan and pour in sufficient oil to come halfway up the sides of the pan. Heat the pan over medium heat until the butter begins to sizzle. To test if the oil is hot enough, sprinkle a few crumbs into it – they should sizzle on contact. Cook the croquettes in batches for 2–3 minutes, turning often, until golden and crisp all over. Remove from the oil using a slotted spoon and drain on kitchen paper to remove excess oil. Serve warm with the mustard on the side. **Pictured on page 50.**

indian potato curry with toor dhal

125 g yellow lentils

3 tablespoons vegetable oil

½ teaspoon mustard seeds

½ teaspoon fenugreek seeds

1 teaspoon grated fresh ginger

1 teaspoon crushed garlic

1 teaspoon chilli powder

1½ teaspoons ground coriander

½ teaspoon ground turmeric

4 tomatoes, skinned and chopped

1 teaspoon salt

750 g floury potatoes, cut into 2-cm chunks

sea salt and freshly ground black pepper

to serve

2 tablespoons freshly chopped coriander, plus extra sprigs

½ teaspoon garam masala

basmati rice

serves 4

Wash the lentils well in several changes of water. Heat the oil in a large saucepan over low heat. Add the mustard and fenugreek seeds. When they begin to pop, stir in the ginger and garlic and fry for 30 seconds.

Add the chilli powder, ground coriander and turmeric and stir-fry for a further 30 seconds. Add the tomatoes and lentils, cover with 600 ml water, add the salt, then bring to the boil. Reduce the heat, cover and simmer for 20–30 minutes or until the lentils are just soft.

Add the potatoes and simmer over low heat for 10–15 minutes or until the potatoes are tender. Season with salt and pepper.

Serve sprinkled with chopped coriander, garam masala and sprigs of fresh coriander. Basmati rice makes a suitable accompaniment.

The humble spud is fantastic for absorbing the rich flavours of fragrant spices, such as in this curry, which makes a hearty meal with the addition of lentils too. The tortilla may not look that substantial, but thanks to the creamy Taleggio cheese, it packs a super-rich taste punch and is more than enough for four to enjoy as a starter or snack.

potato tortilla with red pepper tapenade

10–12 small, waxy new potatoes, thickly sliced

1 small red onion, roughly chopped

1 tablespoon olive oil

250 ml vegetable stock

a handful of fresh flat leaf parsley, chopped

100 g Taleggio cheese, chopped or torn into large chunks

2 eggs, lightly beaten

red pepper tapenade

1 large red pepper

1 garlic clove, chopped

50 g pine nuts, lightly toasted

2 tablespoons olive oil

50 g Parmesan cheese, finely grated

serves 4

To make the tapenade, preheat the oven to 220ºC (425ºF) Gas 7. Put a baking tray in the oven for a few minutes to heat. Put the red pepper on the tray and cook it in the preheated oven for about 15 minutes, turning often until the skin is starting to blacken and puff up. Transfer it to a clean plastic bag and let cool. When the pepper is cool enough to handle, peel off the skin, discard the seeds, roughly tear or chop the flesh and put it in a food processor. Add the garlic, pine nuts and oil and process until smooth. Spoon into a bowl, add the Parmesan and stir well to combine.

Put the potatoes, onion and olive oil in a frying pan set over high heat and cook for 1 minute. Add the stock and cook for about 10 minutes, until the stock has evaporated and the vegetables start to sizzle in the pan. Stir through the parsley and put the pieces of cheese among the potatoes. Pour the eggs into the pan and cook for 2–3 minutes until they start to puff up around the edges. Give the pan a couple of firm shakes – this will make it easier to get the cooked tortilla out of the pan. Meanwhile, preheat the grill to high. Put the frying pan under the hot grill and cook the tortilla for 1–2 minutes, until the top is golden but still wobbly in the centre. Use a spatula to smear some of the tapenade onto the base of a serving plate and carefully slide the tortilla onto the plate. Cut into 4 slices and eat direct from the plate with extra tapenade on the side.

roasted new potatoes

1 kg small poatoes, unpeeled and scrubbed

3 tablespoons olive oil

2 garlic cloves, whole and unpeeled

a few sprigs of fresh rosemary

serves 4

Preheat the oven to 190°C (375°F) Gas 5.

Cut any big potatoes in half so that they are all roughly the same size. Put them into a large, heavy-based roasting tin. Drizzle a little olive oil over the top. Add the garlic and sprigs of rosemary.

Put the tin into the oven and roast for 20 minutes. Take the tin out of the oven and move the potatoes around with a wooden spoon. Roast a little longer if they are still not ready.

bay-roasted hasselbacks

24 small poatoes, unpeeled and scrubbed

approximately 20 fresh bay leaves, torn in half lengthways

15 g unsalted butter

3 tablespoons olive oil

1–2 garlic cloves, crushed

sea salt flakes and freshly ground black pepper

serves 4–6

Preheat the oven to 190°C (375°F) Gas 5.

To prepare the potatoes, spear each potato lengthways with a skewer about 5 mm from the base, slice widthways across the potato as far as the skewer, then remove the skewer.

Insert a couple of pieces of bay leaf, in each sliced potato. Melt the butter with the oil in a heavy-based roasting tin over moderate heat. Stir in the garlic and gently add the potatoes in a single layer. Move them around for 2–3 minutes to colour slightly, then season with sea salt flakes and black pepper.

Roast the potatoes in the preheated oven for 25–30 minutes until golden brown and tender. As they cook, the potatoes will open out like a fan.

potatoes dauphinoise

1 kg waxy potatoes, thinly sliced

125 g freshly grated Parmesan cheese

freshly grated nutmeg

300 ml double cream

sea salt and freshly ground black pepper

a shallow, ovenproof dish, buttered

serves 6

Preheat the oven to 160°C (325°F) Gas 3.

Layer the potatoes in the dish, seasoning each layer with cheese, nutmeg, salt and pepper. Pour over the cream and sprinkle any remaining cheese over the top. Bake in the preheated oven for about 1 hour or until the potatoes are tender and the top is golden and crisp.

hash browns

25 g butter

1 onion, chopped

600 g large potatoes, peeled and grated

1 egg white, beaten

vegetable oil, for deep frying

sea salt and freshly ground black pepper

makes 16

Heat the butter in a frying pan, then add the onion, cover with a lid and cook over low heat until soft.

Put the potatoes into a large mixing bowl and stir in the softened onions. Stir in the egg white and season generously.

Fill a large saucepan one-third full with vegetable oil. Heat to 190°C (or until a blob of the potato mixture browns within a few seconds).

Roll the potato mixture into walnut-sized balls, then flatten slightly before adding to the hot oil. Fry in batches for 2–3 minutes, until golden brown. Drain on kitchen paper and serve with extra salt, for sprinkling.

Sweet potatoes make an excellent ingredient for soups. When blended they take on a velvety, creamy texture. Here, their sweetness is cut through with some full-on and spicy Asian flavours in the form of a Thai-style pesto, which really brings this soup to life.

sweet potato & coconut soup with thai pesto

Put the oil in a heavy-based saucepan set over medium heat. Add the sweet potato and onion, partially cover with a lid and cook for 15 minutes, stirring often, until they are soft and just starting to turn golden. Increase the heat to high, add the curry paste and stir-fry with the sweet potato for 3–4 minutes so that the pasta cooks and becomes fragrant. Add the stock and coconut milk and bring to the boil. Transfer the mixture to a food processor or blender and whizz until smooth. Return the soup to a clean saucepan.

To make the pesto, put all of the ingredients in a food processor or blender and whizz, occasionally scraping down the sides of the bowl, until you have a chunky green paste and the ingredients are all evenly chopped. Gently reheat the soup, then ladle into warmed serving bowls. Top with a generous spoonful of Thai pesto to serve.

* tip

Sweet potatoes are very versatile and can be substituted in place of white potatoes in most recipes, especially the paler varieties. Store them in a cool, dark, dry place, but they should never be refrigerated, as this causes their centres to harden and their flavour to be impaired.

1 tablespoon light olive oil

500 g sweet potato, peeled and chopped into chunks

1 red onion, chopped

1 tablespoon Thai red curry paste

500 ml vegetable stock

500 ml coconut milk

thai pesto

100 g unsalted peanuts, lightly toasted

2 garlic cloves, chopped

2 teaspoons finely grated fresh ginger

2 large green chillies, deseeded and chopped

a small bunch of fresh coriander

a large handful of fresh mint leaves

a large handful of fresh basil leaves

2 tablespoons light soy sauce or Thai fish sauce

2 tablespoons freshly squeezed lime juice

1 tablespoon soft light brown sugar

serves 4

Sweet potato is wonderful paired with nuts, and these two light bites make the most of that heavenly combination. Golden sesame wedges are served with a peanut dipping sauce for a morcish snack, while macadamia nuts add a great crunch to this roasted sweet potato salad.

sesame sweet potato with peanut dipping sauce

750 g sweet potatoes, well scrubbed but unpeeled, cut lengthways into thick wedges

2 tablespoons olive oil

1 tablespoon sesame oil

1 tablespoon sesame seeds

sea salt

fresh coriander, coarsely torn or chopped, to serve

dipping sauce

2 tablespoons organic peanut butter

1 tablespoon freshly squeezed lime juice

½ red chilli, deseeded and sliced

1 tablespoon soy sauce

1 tablespoon tomato ketchup

sea salt and freshly ground black pepper

serves 6–8

Arrange the sweet potato wedges in a single layer on a baking tray, then sprinkle with the olive and sesame oils, sesame seeds and salt. Roast in a preheated oven at 200°C (400°F) Gas 6 for 35 minutes or until tender (the cooking time will vary depending on the size of the wedges).

Meanwhile, to prepare the dipping sauce, put the peanut butter, lime juice, chilli, soy sauce and tomato ketchup in a food processor, add 4 tablespoons hot water and blend until smooth. Add salt and pepper to taste, then pour into a saucepan and heat gently.

Sprinkle the wedges with the coriander and serve with a separate bowl of the dipping sauce.

Variation To simplify this recipe even further, serve the wedges with shop-bought sweet chilli sauce.

roasted sweet potato & macadamia nut salad

3 sweet potatoes (about 300 g each), peeled

1 tablespoon olive oil

1 teaspoon sea salt flakes

70 g raw macadamia nuts, roughly chopped

200 g baby spinach leaves, washed

dressing

2 tablespoons macadamia or olive oil

1 tablespoon cider vinegar

1 teaspoon wholegrain mustard

sea salt and freshly ground black pepper

serves 4

Preheat the oven to 190°C (375°F) Gas 5.

Cut the sweet potatoes into 2-cm cubes and toss in a bowl with the olive oil and salt flakes. Tip onto a baking tray and roast in the preheated oven for 10 minutes.

Put the macadamia nuts in the bowl and toss with any residual oil. Add to the sweet potatoes and roast in the hot oven for 10 minutes, giving the sweet potatoes 20 minutes in total.

To make the dressing, mix together the macadamia oil, vinegar and mustard in a small bowl. Season to taste with salt and pepper.

Arrange the spinach leaves on a serving platter and top with the sweet potatoes and macadamia nuts. Drizzle or spoon the dressing over the top and serve immediately.

tagine of sweet potato, shallots & carrots

2–3 tablespoons olive oil plus a knob of butter

40 g fresh ginger, peeled and finely chopped or grated

1–2 cinnamon sticks or 1–2 teaspoons ground cinnamon

16 small shallots, peeled and left whole

700 g sweet potato, peeled and cut into bite-sized pieces

2 medium carrots, peeled and cut into bite-sized pieces

175 g ready-to-eat stoned prunes

1 tablespoon dark, runny honey

425 ml vegetable or chicken stock

leaves from a small bunch of fresh coriander, roughly chopped

a few fresh mint leaves, chopped

sea salt and freshly ground black pepper

couscous, to serve (optional)

serves 4–6

Heat the olive oil and butter in a tagine or heavy-based casserole. Add the ginger and cinnamon sticks. Toss in the shallots and when they begin to colour add the sweet potato and the carrots. Sauté for 2–3 minutes, stirring, then add the prunes and the honey. Pour in the stock and bring it to the boil. Reduce the heat, cover and cook gently for about 25 minutes.

Uncover and stir in some of the coriander and mint. Season to taste and reduce the liquid, if necessary, by cooking for a further 2–3 minutes uncovered. The vegetables should be tender and slightly caramelized in a very syrupy sauce. Sprinkle with the remaining coriander and mint and serve immediately with couscous, if liked.

Two hearty, warming dishes: this syrupy, caramelized tagine can be adapted to what you have grown – try it with butternut squash or pumpkin instead of sweet potato, if you prefer. The sweet potato and chicken pie is a great way to recycle leftover roast chicken, as well as use up vegetable gluts. To obtain the stale bread, use the end pieces from sliced loaves and toast them in the oven, alongside the sweet potatoes.

roast sweet potato & chicken pie

1.5 kg sweet potatoes, peeled and cut into chunks

3–4 tablespoons olive oil

3 tablespoons butter

1 onion, diced

100 g bacon, chopped

2 celery sticks, chopped

150 g mushrooms, chopped

2 garlic cloves, crushed

2 teaspoons dried thyme

75–100 g sausages, cooked and chopped

100 g vacuum-packed peeled chestnuts, chopped

a large handful of fresh parsley leaves, chopped

½ a chicken (about 700 g), cooked and meat shredded

125 g stale or toasted bread, broken into small pieces

5 tablespoons milk

180 ml chicken stock or water

sea salt and freshly ground black pepper

a 25–30-cm round baking dish, well buttered

serves 4–6

Preheat the oven to 220°C (425°F) Gas 7.

Toss the sweet potatoes with the olive oil and arrange in a single layer on a baking tray. Roast in the preheated oven for about 45 minutes, until tender and browned. Reduce the oven temperature to 200°C (400°F) Gas 6. Let the sweet potatoes cool, then mash with butter to taste and season with salt. Set aside.

Heat some of the oil in a frying pan. Add the onion and cook for 2–3 minutes, until soft. Season with salt, then add the bacon, celery and mushrooms and cook for 3–5 minutes, stirring often. Add the garlic, thyme, sausage and chestnuts and cook for about 1 minute. Stir in the parsley and chicken and set aside.

In a bowl, combine the bread pieces and milk and toss to coat. The bread should be moist, you may need to add more milk. Add the bread to the chicken mixture, along with the stock. Stir well. Taste and adjust the seasoning.

Spread the chicken mixture in an even layer in the prepared baking dish. It will dry out slightly with baking, so if it seems dry at the outset, add a bit more of any liquid: stock, milk or water. Top with the mashed sweet potato, spread evenly. Bake in the preheated oven for about 45 minutes. (The sweet potato won't brown but should start to blacken slightly where peaked.)

The delicate flavour of carrots is best blended with vegetable stock or water as chicken muddies the flavour of really good carrots. However, if you're doubtful of your carrots' flavour, go for a good chicken stock.

spiced carrot soup

50 g butter

1 onion, chopped

800 g carrots, chopped

2 teaspoons ground coriander

½ teaspoon ground ginger

¼ teaspoon chilli powder

1 litre vegetable stock or water

4 tablespoons double cream

2 tablespoons sunflower oil

5-cm piece fresh ginger, cut into matchsticks

sea salt and freshly ground black pepper

serves 4

Melt the butter in a large saucepan and sauté the onion for 5–8 minutes until softened. Add the carrots, coriander, ground ginger and chilli powder and stir into the butter to coat them and release the flavour of the spices. Season well, then pour in the stock. Simmer for 40 minutes.

Transfer the contents of the pan to a blender in batches (or use a handheld blender) and liquidize to a smooth purée. Stir in the cream. Add a little more water if it is too thick and season to taste.

Heat the sunflower oil in a frying pan over high heat and fry the ginger for 1 minute, or until crisp.

Divide the soup equally between 4 bowls, garnish with the fried ginger and serve.

roasted carrots with barley risotto

2 tablespoons light olive oil

12 baby carrots, ends trimmed

50 g butter

2 sprigs of fresh thyme

2 garlic cloves, unpeeled and cut in half

500 ml chicken stock

1 tablespoon light soy sauce

220 g barley

3 heaped tablespoons finely grated Parmesan cheese

sea salt and freshly ground black pepper

serves 4

Heat the oil in a frying pan until very hot. Add the carrots and cook for 8–10 minutes, turning every 2 minutes, until golden. If your pan isn't big enough you may need to do this in batches. Add 30 g of the butter, the thyme and garlic to the pan with 125 ml water and season with sea salt and black pepper. Cover the pan with a tight-fitting lid and cook over medium heat for 15–20 minutes, turning often, until the carrots are tender.

Meanwhile, to make the barley risotto, put the stock and soy sauce in a saucepan with 1 litre water and bring to the boil. Add the barley and cook for 45–50 minutes, stirring often, until the barley is soft but not breaking up. Stir in the remaining butter and Parmesan. Serve the carrots on top of the barley.

Variation The carrots could be served hot on a bed of couscous or left to cool and tossed in a salad with beetroot, toasted pine nuts and a soft cheese.

Barley is a wonderful ingredient – it's so earthy and and can enhance all sorts of dishes. It's used here to make a dish much like a risotto, but without all the stirring! Miso and Parmesan work well together and give the barley an intensely savoury flavour that is perfect with sweet new season carrots.

madeira-glazed roast carrots

750 g young carrots
1 tablespoon olive oil
50 g unsalted butter
1 teaspoon sugar
125 ml Madeira wine
sea salt and freshly ground black pepper

a handful of fresh flat leaf parsley, corsely chopped, to serve

serves 4–6

Wash and trim the carrots. If large, cut into 4-cm chunks, but if small or medium, leave them whole. Par-boil them in a large saucepan of boiling water for about 10 minutes, leaving them still slightly hard in the middle. Drain.

Meanwhile, heat the oil and butter in a roasting tin in a preheated oven at 200°C (400°F) Gas 6 until the butter begins to brown. Add the carrots, turn to coat in the oil, then sprinkle with salt, pepper and the sugar and return to the oven for 10 minutes. Turn them and roast for a further 15 minutes. Add the Madeira and cook until all the liquid has gone. Serve sprinkled with parsley.

spiced carrot dip

250 ml vegetable stock
4 medium carrots, chopped
2 tablespoons light olive oil
1 small red onion, chopped
2 garlic cloves, chopped
1 large red chilli, chopped

1 teaspoon fenugreek seeds
1 teaspoon ground cumin
sea salt and white pepper

serves 6–8

Put the stock in a saucepan and add the carrots, oil, onion, and garlic. Bring to the boil, then reduce the heat to low and simmer for 15–20 minutes, until almost all the liquid has evaporated and the carrots are soft. Add the chilli, fenugreek seeds and cumin and stir-fry for 2–3 minutes.

Transfer the mixture to a food processor or blender and whizz until blended but still with a rough texture. Season to taste, transfer to a serving dish and cover until ready to serve.

carrots with cream & herbs

800 g baby carrots, or medium carrots
50 g unsalted butter
a sprig of fresh thyme
2 tablespoons crème fraîche
several sprigs of fresh chervil, snipped

a small bunch of fresh chives, snipped
fine sea salt

serves 4

Trim the carrots (or if using larger carrots, cut them diagonally into 5-cm slices). Put them in a large saucepan (the carrots should fit in almost a single layer for even cooking). Add the butter and set over low heat. Cook for 3 minutes, until the butter has melted and coated the carrots. Half fill the saucepan with water, then add a pinch of salt and the thyme. Cover and cook for 10–20 minutes, until the water is almost completely evaporated.

Stir in the crème fraîche and add sea salt to taste. Sprinkle the herbs over the top. Mix well and serve.

vichy carrots with fresh ginger

1 kg carrots
2 tablespoons finely chopped fresh ginger
50 g unsalted butter
½ teaspoon sea salt
2 teaspoons caster sugar

freshly ground black pepper
3 tablespoons freshly chopped coriander or parsley

serves 8

Cut the carrots into batons or thick rounds and put in a saucepan with the ginger, butter, salt and sugar. Half-cover with water, bring to the boil and boil steadily, stirring once or twice, until the water has almost disappeared and the carrots are tender.

Reduce the heat and let the carrots brown a little and caramelize. Season with black pepper and stir in the coriander or parsley. Serve immediately.

carrot & walnut cake
with cream cheese filling

Carrots contain plenty of natural sugars and so are perfect for sweet dishes, such as a classic carrot cake. This version adds walnuts too, and is wonderfully crumbly and soft – and probably best eaten with a spoon! If you are nervous about cutting the cake through the centre, simply spread the creamy filling over the top of the cooled cake instead.

2 eggs, separated

110 g raw (unrefined) sugar

200 ml light olive oil

1 teaspoon bicarbonate of soda

185 g plain flour

2 teaspoons baking powder

1 teaspoon ground cinnamon

¼ teaspoon freshly grated nutmeg

200 g grated carrot

100 g walnut halves

cream cheese filling

250 g cream cheese

125 g butter, cubed

3 tablespoons brown sugar

2–3 tablespoons maple syrup

a 20-cm diameter springform cake tin, lightly greased

serves 8

Preheat the oven to 180°C (350°F) Gas 4.

Put the egg yolks and raw sugar in a large bowl and beat for 2 minutes. Add the oil and bicarbonate of soda and beat until just combined. Fold in the flour, spices, carrot and walnuts until combined. The mixture should look quite thick. In a separate grease-free bowl, beat the egg whites with an electric whisk until they form soft peaks then fold them into the cake mixture in 2 batches. Spoon the cake mixture into the prepared cake tin and bake in the preheated oven for 45–50 minutes, until golden and slightly puffed on top. Let the cake cool in the tin for about 10 minutes before turning it out onto a wire rack.

To make the filling, put the cream cheese and butter in a bowl and let them come to room temperature. Add the brown sugar and, using an electric whisk, beat for 5 minutes, until there are no lumps and the beaters leave a trail when turned off. Add the maple syrup a little at a time and beat for a further 2 minutes, until the mixture is smooth and a spreadable consistency. Carefully slice the cooled cake in half and spread the filling on the bottom layer.

Parsnips make a wonderful soup ingredient, sweet and warming, and preparing them in this way is especially good if they are slightly woody. They have a very distinctive taste which marries well with the sweetness of apples, and the flavours are enhanced by a pinch of spicy curry powder and some fresh thyme. The chorizo recipe is a thick and unctuous soup; the kind you could wolf down after a long walk or building a snowman in the depths of winter. It's very heavy so a little goes a long way; serve it as a meal in itself – offering it as a starter is likely to leave anyone too stuffed for a follow-up course. Both recipes are just the thing to brighten up a dreary winter's day.

parsnip, chorizo & chestnut soup

125 g raw chorizo, cubed

1 onion, chopped

3 garlic cloves, sliced

1 celery stick, chopped

1 carrot, chopped

3 parsnips, chopped

¼ teaspoon dried chilli flakes

1 teaspoon ground cumin

200 g peeled, cooked chestnuts (fresh or vacuum-packed)

1 litre hot chicken or ham stock

sea salt and freshly ground black pepper

serves 4–6

Put the chorizo in a large saucepan and heat gently for 2–3 minutes until the oil seeps out and the chorizo becomes slightly crispy. Lift out the chorizo with a slotted spoon, trying to leave as much oil behind as you can and set to one side.

Add the onion, garlic, celery, carrot and parsnips to the pan, stir well, cover and cook gently for 10 minutes, or until softening. Add the chilli flakes and cumin, season with sea salt and freshly ground black pepper and stir to release the aroma. Add the chestnuts and hot stock, then cover and simmer over low heat for 25–30 minutes until everything is very tender.

Transfer the contents of the pan to a blender (or use a handheld blender) and liquidize until smooth. Reheat the chorizo in a small frying pan.

Divide the soup equally between 4–6 bowls, scatter with the crispy chorizo and serve.

parsnip, apple & thyme soup

1 small onion, chopped

2 tablespoons olive oil

1 teaspoon mild curry powder

a few sprigs of fresh thyme

450 g parsnips (about 2–3), peeled and chopped

1 large tart cooking apple, such as Bramley, peeled, cored and roughly chopped

1.25 litres chicken or vegetable stock

1 tablespoon unsalted butter

3 heaped tablespoons crème fraîche, plus extra to serve

sea salt and freshly ground black pepper

croûtons, to serve (optional)

serves 4

Put the onions, oil, curry powder and a good pinch of salt in a large saucepan. Cook gently over low heat until the onions are soft. Add the thyme, parsnips and apple and stir well. Cook for about 5 minutes, adding a little more oil if it needs it and stirring often. Add the stock and season to taste.

Simmer gently, uncovered, until the parsnips are soft, about 15–20 minutes. Purée the soup with a handheld blender, or by transferring it to a food processor and returning to the saucepan once blended. Taste and adjust the seasoning if necessary.

Stir in the butter and 3 heaped tablespoons crème fraîche and mix well. Ladle the soup into serving bowls and top with croûtons (if using) and a small dollop of crème fraîche.

honey-roast parsnip, carrot & shallot tart

200 g carrots, sliced on the diagonal

200 g parsnips, cut into matchsticks

180 g shallots, halved or quartered, depending on their size

1 tablespoon runny honey

40 ml olive oil

1 teaspoon salt

½ teaspoon crushed black pepper

100 g mature Cheddar, grated

150 g Greek yoghurt

spelt pizza dough base

220 g wholemeal spelt flour

1 teaspoon dried quick yeast

½ teaspoon salt

2 tablespoons olive oil

1 egg

60 ml warm water

a 23-cm loose-based tart tin, greased

makes about 8 slices

Plenty of roasted winter vegetables with a hint of honey set in a light wholemeal spelt and olive oil pastry – this makes a great rustic starter or accompaniment to winter roasts and stews.

Preheat the oven to 200ºC (400ºF) Gas 6.

Put the carrots, parsnips and shallots in a roasting tray. Add the honey, oil, salt and pepper and toss until evenly coated. Cover the tray with aluminium foil and roast in the preheated oven for 30 minutes. Remove from the oven, leave covered, and leave to cool for 10–15 minutes.

Reduce the oven temperature to 170ºC (325ºF) Gas 3.

To make the pastry, mix the flour, yeast and salt in a bowl. Make a well in the centre and pour in the oil, egg and water. Draw everything together with your hands until you get a soft dough.

Transfer the dough to a lightly floured surface and knead for a couple of minutes. The dough should be soft but not sticky. If it is sticky, add a little flour and knead again. Roll out the dough with a rolling pin until 3 mm thick. Line the tart tin with the dough but do not trim the edges yet.

Mix 60 g of the cheese into the roasted vegetables.

Mix together the yoghurt and remaining cheese in a bowl, then spoon into the tart shell.

Scatter the roasted vegetables over the yoghurt, spreading them evenly. Now trim the excess pizza dough neatly around the edges.

Bake in the hot oven for 25–30 minutes. Remove from the oven and leave to cool.

Earthy and fruity, with a hint of ginger, this tagine is a good winter warmer. It can be made with either fresh or pre-cooked beetroot. You could serve it with roasted butternut squash and a mound of couscous tossed with pistachios. With a summer crop, prepare a pretty cardinals' salad, so called because the colours are reminiscent of a cardinal's ruby-red robes. The sweetness of the beetroot contrasts well with the bitterness of the radicchio leaves. You could also add some potatoes for a more substantial salad.

beetroot & beef tagine with oranges

1–2 tablespoons ghee, or 1 tablespoon olive oil plus a knob of butter

3–4 garlic cloves, crushed

1 red onion, halved lengthways and sliced with the grain

40 g fresh ginger, peeled and finely chopped or grated

1 red chilli, deseeded and sliced

2 teaspoons coriander seeds, crushed

2 cinnamon sticks

3–4 beetroots, peeled and quartered

500 g lean beef, cut into bite-sized cubes or strips

2 thin-skinned oranges, cut into segments

1 tablespoon dark, runny honey

1–2 tablespoons orange flower water

a knob of butter

2–3 tablespoons shelled pistachios

leaves from a small bunch of fresh flat leaf parsley, roughly chopped

sea salt and freshly ground black pepper

couscous, to serve

serves 4–6

Melt the ghee in a tagine or heavy-based casserole, add the garlic, onion and ginger and stir until they begin to colour. Add the chilli, coriander seeds and cinnamon sticks. Add the beetroot and sauté for 2–3 minutes. Toss in the beef and sauté for 1 minute. Pour in enough water to almost cover the beef and beetroot and bring to the boil. Reduce the heat, cover with a lid and simmer for 1 hour, until the meat is very tender.

Add the orange segments, honey and orange flower water to the tagine and season to taste with salt and pepper. Cover with the lid and cook for a further 10–15 minutes.

Melt the butter in a small saucepan and toss in the pistachios, stirring them over medium heat until they turn golden brown. Sprinkle them over the tagine along with the flat leaf parsley and serve immediately with couscous.

cardinal's salad

4 tablespoons mayonnaise

1 tablespoon red wine vinegar or raspberry vinegar

2 tablespoons extra virgin olive oil

3 tablespoons chopped fresh chives

1 head radicchio, shredded

500 g cooked beetroot, thinly sliced

½ cucmber, thinly sliced

a bunch of radishes, quartered

3 eggs, hard-bolled and quartered

freshly ground black pepper

serves 6

Put the mayonnaise, vinegar and olive oil in a bowl and stir to mix. Stir in half the chives and set aside.

Arrange the shredded radicchio on a serving platter. Add a layer of beetroot and a spoonful of the mayonnaise dressing. Add a layer of cucumber and another spoonful of dressing.

Top with the radishes, then the eggs. Drizzle over the remaining dressing, sprinkle with black pepper and the remaining chives and serve.

If you have a glut of beetroot, it makes the perfect base for preserves. Sweet, sour and delicately spiced, this gorgeous chutney is perfect for serving with heavier cheeses and crackers. If you're serving burgers, sausages or steaks (even salmon steaks), beetroot & horseradish relish will transform the meal. Fresh, raw beetroot is best, but you can substitute pre-cooked if you are short on time.

beetroot, fennel & apple chutney

160 g cooked beetroot, diced

150 g fennel, trimmed and diced

150 g sour apple, peeled, cored and diced

100 g red onion, diced

190 ml spirit vinegar

220 g golden caster sugar

½ star anise

2 cloves

1 teaspoon salt

2 x 250-g jars, sterilized (see note on page 4)

makes two 250-g jars

Put all the ingredients in a saucepan and bring to the boil, then cook over medium heat for 1 hour, stirring occasionally. If after 1 hour the chutney hasn't reached a jam-like consistency, leave it to cook for up to 20 more minutes.

Spoon the hot chutney into the sterilized jars and seal immediately. Leave for 2–3 days before serving. The chutney will keep in the refrigerator for up to 2 weeks.

beetroot & horseradish relish

2 tablespoons sugar

2 tablespoons balsamic vinegar

300 g raw beetroot, peeled

1 tablespoon bottled horseradish

makes 300 ml

To make the relish, put the sugar and vinegar in a small saucepan and bring to the boil, stirring. Boil for 1 minute, then remove from the heat. Grate the beetroot into a bowl and combine with the horseradish and vinegar syrup. The relish will keep in the refrigerator for up to 1 week.

 tip

Beetroot can be enjoyed both raw (they are delicious grated into salads) and cooked. If cooking, always leave the skins on while doing so as this will preserve more of the colour and nutrients in the vegetable. After cooking, the thin skins can be easily rubbed off under running water.

mini chocolate, beetroot & cherry cakes

75 g dark chocolate
(about 50% cocoa solids)

175 g self-raising flour

40 g cocoa powder

175 g light muscovado or light
brown soft sugar

250 ml groundnut or vegetable
oil

3 large eggs

a pinch of salt

150 g cooked, peeled beetroot

50 g dried sour cherries
(or dried cranberries), roughly
chopped

*a 9-hole petite loaf tin (base
measurement of each hole
5.5 x 8 cm and 2.5 cm deep),
lined with mini-loaf cases*

makes 9

Preheat the oven to 180°C (350°F) Gas 4.

Break the chocolate into pieces and melt it in a heatproof bowl set over a pan of barely simmering water. Leave to cool slightly.

Sift the flour into an electric mixer (or use a large mixing bowl and an electric whisk). Add the cocoa, sugar, oil, eggs, salt and the melted chocolate, and whisk until combined. Using the coarse side of a grater, grate the beetroot into the mixture and sprinkle in the chopped sour cherries. Using a large metal spoon, fold everything together gently.

Divide the mixture between the loaf cases. Bake in the preheated oven for 20–25 minutes, or until well risen. Leave the cakes to cool completely in the tin.

Note The petite loaf tin and matching cases needed for these cakes can be bought from www.janeasher.co.uk. If you prefer, you can bake the cakes in muffin cases instead of mini-loaf cases – they will take 25–30 minutes in the oven, and make 9 muffins.

Using beetroot in these cakes gives them slightly squidgy centres and they freeze well, before decorating. They are also lovely to make as a gift, just dust the tops with cocoa, then sprinkle with edible mini gold balls – dip the end of your finger in a little cold water before applying so that they stick.

beetroot **33**

bulb & stem vegetables

braised fennel with polenta ❧ fennel roasted in butter

fennel & lemon risotto ❧ fennel & tomato focaccia

leek & potato soup ❧ flamiche

sage buttered baby leeks with chilli breadcrumbs

charred leeks with tarator sauce ❧ grilled asparagus

with baby chorizo ❧ cream of asparagus soup

asparagus & goats' cheese tart ❧ asparagus tagliatelle

mediterranean stuffed onions with rice

french onion soup ❧ roasted onions & sausages

crispy onion rings ❧ braised onions ❧ pickled onions

Don't be too quick to trim away the feathery leaves from fennel bulbs – these can be added to the final stages of a dish or used as a garnish. While smaller, tender bulbs can be eaten raw, the larger, tougher ones are perfect when braised, as here. Or try roasting fennel bulbs in butter, which transforms them into a perfect accompaniment for any roast, especially fish.

braised fennel with polenta

2 large fennel bulbs
65 ml light olive oil
1 onion, chopped
2 garlic cloves, chopped
1 small red chilli, chopped
a handful of fresh flat leaf parsley leaves, roughly chopped
2 tablespoons freshly squeezed lemon juice
2 tablespoons sweet white wine
500 ml vegetable stock

a handful of small black olives
grated pecorino cheese, to serve

creamy polenta

500 ml full-fat milk
1 litre vegetable stock
200 g instant polenta
50 g butter
100 g pecorino cheese, finely grated

serves 4

Cut about ½ cm from the gnarly stem on the bottom of the fennel bulbs. Cut off the fronds, chop finely and reserve. Cut off and discard all but about 1 cm from the dark green stems. Thinly slice the remaining white fennel bulb lengthways. Put the oil in a heavy-based saucepan and set over high heat. Add the onion, garlic and chillies and cook for 2–3 minutes until softened. Add the parsley and fennel bulb and fronds and cook for 2–3 minutes, stirring often so that the fennel becomes coated in the oil. Add the lemon juice, wine and stock and bring to the boil. Cover with a lid and turn the heat down to a low simmer for 20 minutes, stirring occasionally. Add the olives, remove the lid and boil rapidly until there is only a little liquid left and the fennel is very soft.

Meanwhile, to make the polenta, put the milk and stock in a saucepan and bring to a gentle simmer over medium heat. Slowly pour in the polenta in a steady stream and beat with a balloon whisk until smooth. Reduce the heat to low and continue to beat for 2–3 minutes. When the mixture thickens, discard the whisk and use a wooden spoon. Add the butter and cheese and stir until melted into the polenta. Spoon some polenta onto serving plates, top with the braised fennel and sprinkle with grated pecorino to serve.

fennel roasted in butter

3 fennel bulbs
4 tablespoons olive oil or melted butter
sea salt

freshly chopped dill, tarragon or fennel fronds (optional), to serve

serves 6

Trim and remove the stalks and coarse outer leaves from the fennel if necessary. Cut each bulb in half, then each half into 2–3 pieces, depending on size. Slice each piece with a bit of stem or root attached to keep the pieces in place. Reserve any feathery fronds, to chop over the dish just before serving.

Put the fennel in a large saucepan of lightly salted water, bring to the boil and blanch until nearly tender. Drain and pat dry.

Arrange the pieces in a single layer in a roasting tin, baste with the oil or butter and cook in a preheated oven at 220°C (425°F) Gas 7 for about 20 minutes. From time to time, turn them and baste with the oil or butter so they brown evenly on all sides.

To enhance the aniseed flavour, dust with chopped dill, tarragon or fennel fronds, if using, then serve.

Variation Sprinkle with cheese and cook for a further 5 minutes, then serve as a separate dish or starter.

fennel

fennel & lemon risotto

a small pinch of saffron threads

1.25 litres hot vegetable stock

1 large fennel bulb

125 g butter

1 onion, chopped

2 garlic cloves

freshly squeezed juice and grated zest of 1 unwaxed lemon

300 g risotto rice

100 ml vodka

50 g freshly grated Parmesan cheese

sea salt and freshly ground black pepper

serves 4

Soak the saffron in the hot stock until required. Finely chop the fennel bulb and fronds, reserving the fronds.

Melt half the butter in a frying pan, add the onion, chopped fennel, garlic and lemon zest and fry gently for 10 minutes until softened. Add the rice and stir for 30 seconds until the grains are glossy.

Meanwhile, heat the saffron stock to a gentle simmer. Add a ladle of the stock to the rice and cook, stirring until absorbed. Continue adding the stock a little at a time, stirring, and cook for about 20 minutes until the liquid is absorbed and the rice is al dente (just done).

Remove the pan from the heat, stir in the remaining butter, lemon juice, vodka, Parmesan, reserved fennel fronds, salt and pepper, cover, leave for 5 minutes, then serve.

Adding a nip of vodka towards the end of cooking adds a delightful flavour to this fennel & lemon risotto. This recipe is simple to make and always a terrific success with guests. Also great for lunchtime visitors is Focaccia – a rustic-style bread traditionally cooked over an open fire and made for tearing and sharing. If you like this recipe, try it again topped with other ingredients such as red onions, olives and sprigs of rosemary or thyme.

fennel & tomato focaccia

2 baby fennel bulbs, thinly sliced and fronds chopped

2 tomatoes, thinly sliced

1½ teaspoons sea salt flakes

extra virgin olive oil, to serve

1 teaspoon salt

2 teaspoons dried yeast

3 tablespoons olive oil

plain flour, for kneading and dusting

focaccia dough

450 g strong white bread flour

serves 6–8

For the dough, sift the flour and salt into a large bowl and add the yeast. Stir to combine and make a small well in the centre. Add 300 ml warm water and 2 tablespoons of the olive oil. Quickly stir a few times just to combine, then use your hands to bring the mixture together. (If the mixture is sticking to your hands, add a little flour, but avoid using it if at all possible.) Transfer the dough to a lightly floured surface and knead for 8–10 minutes, until smooth and elastic. Form the dough into a ball and put it in a lightly oiled bowl. Cover with a tea towel and let sit in a warm place for 1½ hours, until doubled in size.

Preheat the oven to 220ºC (425ºF) Gas 7. Put the ball of dough on a lightly oiled baking tray. Using a lightly floured rolling pin, gently roll from the centre upwards in one motion, not pressing too firmly so that any air bubbles stay intact. Roll from the centre down to the opposite end to form a rough oval shape, about 30 cm long and 20 cm at its widest point. Lightly cover and let sit again for 20–30 minutes until it has risen.

Use the tips of your fingers to press dimples over the surface of the dough. Lay the fennel and tomato slices on top and scatter with the fronds. Drizzle with the remaining olive oil and sprinkle with the salt flakes. Bake in the preheated oven for 25 minutes. Carefully slide the focaccia off the tray and put it directly on the oven shelf. Cook for a further 5 minutes, until the crust is golden. Remove from the oven and leave to cool before eating. Serve with a small bowl of fruity extra virgin olive oil for dipping.

Sometimes the classics really are the best, and with both leek and potato soup and a traditional flamiche tart from Belgium, this is certainly true. While the soup is a perfect winter warmer, the tart is ideal for a picnic served with some pâté and cold meats. If your leeks are from the garden, complete with the mud and insects that cohabit with them, place them in a sink full of warm water and swirl them around to dissolve the mud and encourage it to come out.

leek & potato soup

50 g butter

4 leeks (about 500 g), chopped

3 potatoes, peeled and chopped (about 250 g)

1 onion, finely chopped

500 ml vegetable stock

300 ml milk

2 dried bay leaves

2 tablespoons freshly snipped chives, to serve

sea salt and freshly ground black pepper

serves 4–6

Melt the butter in a large, preferably heavy-based saucepan and add the leeks, potatoes, onion and a large pinch of salt. Cover and cook over low heat for 15 minutes until soft and translucent. Stir occasionally so that the vegetables don't catch.

Add the stock, milk and bay leaves and bring to the boil. Turn the heat down and simmer, covered, for 20 minutes until the potato is so soft it is falling apart.

Transfer the soup to a blender, removing the bay leaves as you unearth them, and liquidize until smooth. Strain the blended soup back into the pan to get it extra smooth. Bring back to the boil.

Divide the soup between 4–6 bowls and scatter with chives and a fresh grinding of black pepper.

flamiche

350 g ready-made shortcrust pastry, at room temperature

75 g butter

900 g leeks, split, well washed and thickly sliced

1 teaspoon salt

4 egg yolks

300 ml double cream or crème fraîche

freshly grated nutmeg, to taste

sea salt and freshly ground black pepper

a 20.5-cm diameter tart tin

a baking tray

foil or baking paper and baking beans

serves 4–6

Preheat the oven to 200°C (400°F) Gas 6.

Roll out the pastry thinly on a lightly floured work surface, then use it to line the tart tin, prick the base, then chill or freeze for 15 minutes. After this time, line the tin with foil or baking paper then fill with baking beans. Bake in the centre of the oven for 10–12 minutes. Remove the foil or baking paper and baking beans and return the pie crust to the oven for 5–7 minutes longer to dry out completely.

For the tart filling, melt the butter in a large saucepan and add the leeks, stirring to coat. Add a few tablespoons of water and the 1 teaspoon salt, and cover with a lid. Steam very gently for at least 30 minutes (trying not to look too often!) until soft and melting. Remove the lid and cook for a further few minutes to evaporate any excess liquid – the mixture should be quite thick. Leave to cool.

Put the egg yolks and cream or crème fraîche into a bowl, add salt, pepper and nutmeg to taste and beat well. Set the pastry case on a baking tray. Spoon the cooled leeks evenly into the pastry case, fluffing them up a bit with a fork. Pour the eggs and cream mixture over the top.

Bake in the preheated oven for 30 minutes or until set and pale golden brown. Serve warm.

Sage makes a great partnership with leeks, and the Italian-style chilli breadcrumb topping makes for a delicious combination. For an even more pronounced Italian accent, the crispy breadcrumbs are made from ciabatta bread. For a Middle Eastern flavour, top barbecued leeks with a nut sauce, tarator. This recipe uses macadamias, though traditionally it is prepared with ground almonds or walnuts. If the sauce is made in advance, whisk well before use.

charred leeks
with tarator sauce

750 g baby leeks, trimmed

2–3 tablespoons extra virgin olive oil

sea salt

a few lemon wedges, to serve

2 garlic cloves, crushed

100 ml extra virgin olive oil

1 tablespoon lemon juice

2 tablespoons boiling water

sea salt and freshly ground black pepper

tarator sauce

50 g macadamia nuts, toasted

25 g fresh breadcrumbs

serves 4

To make the sauce, put the nuts into a food processor and grind coarsely, then add the breadcrumbs, garlic, salt and pepper and process again to form a smooth paste. Transfer to a bowl and very gradually whisk in the olive oil, lemon juice and the 2 tablespoons boiling water to form a sauce. Season to taste with salt and pepper.

Preheat the barbecue. Brush the leeks with a little olive oil, season with salt and cook over medium hot coals for 6–10 minutes, turning occasionally, until charred and tender. Transfer to a serving plate, sprinkle with olive oil, then pour the sauce over the top and serve with the lemon wedges.

sage buttered baby leeks
with chilli breadcrumbs

75 g salted butter

2 tablespoons finely chopped fresh sage

500 g short thin baby leeks, split halfway through and well washed

2 tablespoons extra virgin olive oil

50 g fresh ciabatta breadcrumbs

1 mild long red chilli, deseeded and finely chopped

1 smaller red chilli, deseeded and sliced into rings

serves 4

Put the butter and sage in a bowl and mash well.

Steam or boil the leeks for about 5 minutes, or until tender. Toss in half the sage butter and keep hot.

Heat a frying pan, add the olive oil and ciabatta breadcrumbs and fry for about 45 seconds. Add the remaining sage butter and the finely chopped chillies. Fry until golden.

Put the leeks on a serving plate, and top with the chilli breadcrumbs and the smaller sliced chilli. Serve with other dishes or as a starter.

Note Sea kale and salsify are also good served this way.

Asparagus is a vegetable much used in Spanish cuisine, and this heritage is illustrated in these two dishes. Asparagus served with fresh mayonnaise, coarse sea salt and sautéed sliced baby chorizos is a simple rustic country dish. Asparagus soup has a delicate flavour that goes very well with sherry – try a manzanilla with this dish.

grilled asparagus with baby chorizo

750 g thin asparagus
3 tablespoons olive oil
a pinch of fine sea salt
freshly ground black pepper

mayonnaise

1 garlic clove, finely chopped
2 teaspoons freshly squeezed lemon juice
a pinch of salt

1 egg yolk
150 ml olive oil

to serve

coarse sea salt

2 baby chorizos (choricitos), sliced, then fried without oil in a dry frying pan

serves 4

To make the mayonnaise, put the garlic, half the lemon juice, a pinch of salt and a few drops of water in a mortar and pound to a paste. Add the egg yolk, grinding with the pestle in one direction. Gradually mix in the oil in drops. After adding 100 ml, add a little more of the lemon juice and continue slowly mixing in the oil until a thick emulsion forms. Taste and adjust the flavour with more salt and the remaining lemon juice if needed. Alternatively, use a blender or small food processor, but you will have to double the ingredients or the mixture won't cover the blades. Cover any leftovers with clingfilm, chill and keep for another use.

Trim the asparagus and peel away the papery triangular bits from the stalk. Put the oil, salt and pepper in a shallow dish, add the asparagus and turn to coat.

Heat a ridged stove-top grill pan until smoking. Add the asparagus, a batch at a time, turning the spears over when grill marks appear. They will take 1½–2½ minutes on each side. Serve while still hot with the mayonnaise, sea salt and chorizos in small bowls.

cream of asparagus soup

750 g asparagus
3 tablespoons olive oil
1 tablespoon butter
2 leeks, well washed and thinly sliced
1 onion, finely chopped

1 litre chicken stock
freshly grated nutmeg
150 ml double cream
fine sea salt and freshly ground white pepper

serves 4

Cut the tips off 8 asparagus spears and reserve. Chop the remainder into 2-cm pieces.

Heat the oil and butter in a saucepan, add the leeks and onion, cover and sauté over gentle heat for 10 minutes. Add the chopped asparagus, stock, grated nutmeg, season well with salt and pepper and simmer for 10 minutes.

Transfer to a blender, purée until smooth, then, using the back of a ladle, push through a sieve set over a bowl. Alternatively, use a mouli. Add two-thirds of the cream to the bowl and stir well. Return the soup to the saucepan and heat gently when ready to serve (do not let boil).

Cook the reserved asparagus tips in boiling water until just tender. Ladle the soup into bowls, spoon the remaining cream on top, add the asparagus tips and some more nutmeg, then serve.

There must be something extremely special about asparagus for it to survive being called names like 'chambermaids' horror' and 'sparrows' guts'! Young asparagus is one of life's great gifts, but don't miss its short seasonal window, especially the British asparagus season which really kicks off in May and ends in June. Because it is such a treat, keep it simple. Of course it is wonderful served with hollandaise, but try combining the prime spears with a handful of other fresh, good-quality ingredients. It is a perfect foil for rich ingredients, such as the goats' cheese in this tart and a creamy pasta.

asparagus & goats' cheese tart

2 x 375-g sheets ready-rolled puff pastry, defrosted if frozen

1 egg, lightly beaten and mixed with 2 teaspoons water

2 tablespoons butter

2 tablespoons light olive oil

2 bunches thin asparagus, woody ends trimmed

150 g soft goats' cheese

sea salt and freshly ground black pepper

2 baking trays, lined with baking paper

serves 4

Preheat the oven to 220°C (425°F) Gas 7. Cut the sheets of pastry to make two rectangles 24 x 12 cm and place each one on a baking tray lined with baking paper. Cut 1-cm wide strips from the remaining pastry. Brush around the edges of the pastry rectangles and place the strips on the edges to form a border. Prick the centre of each pastry with a fork and brush the beaten egg all over it. Cook in the preheated oven for 15 minutes, until pale golden and puffed.

Put the butter and olive oil in a frying pan over high heat and cook the asparagus for 2–3 minutes, turning often, until just beginning to soften. Season well with sea salt and black pepper and set aside. Crumble the goats' cheese over the pastry, staying within the borders. Top with the asparagus and cook in the oven for a further 10 minutes until the pastry is dark golden. Serve warm.

asparagus tagliatelle

250 ml single cream

300 g tagliatelle pasta, or simliar

1 bunch of fine asparagus, trimmed and each spear cut into 4

grated zest and freshly squeezed juice of 1 unwaxed lemon

3 tablespoons finely chopped fresh flat leaf parsley

100 g finely grated Parmesan cheese

sea salt and freshly ground black pepper

serves 4, as a starter

Put the cream in a small saucepan and bring to the boil. Reduce the heat to a low simmer and cook for 8–10 minutes, until slightly thickened. Set aside.

Cook the pasta according to the packet instructions. About 2 minutes before the pasta is cooked, add the asparagus to the boiling water. Drain well and return to the warm pan with the reduced cream, lemon zest and juice, parsley and half of the Parmesan. Toss together, season well with sea salt and black pepper and serve with the remaining cheese sprinkled on top.

Variation As a substitute to asparagus, pan-fry 1 grated courgette in 1 tablespoon of butter over medium heat until softened and golden. Add the courgette to the well-drained pasta along with the other ingredients.

Onions are easy to grow in abundance and these recipes make sure you get through plenty of them. Both dishes are warming and comforting. Onions make a nifty, and tasty, container for the gently spiced lamb filling. Rich French onion soup, topped with melting cheese toasts is synonymous with bistro eating. This recipe is a simplified version, the sort of thing that's ideal when it's chilly outside, people are hungry inside and there's not much more than a few onions lurking about.

mediterranean stuffed onions with rice

8 large red or white onions

2–3 tablespoons olive oil

500 g lamb mince

2 garlic cloves, crushed

1 heaped tablespoon tomato purée

125 ml dry white wine

½ teaspoon ground cinnamon

2 tablespoons finely chopped fresh dill

2 tablespoons finely chopped fresh mint

300 g brown rice

100 g fresh breadcrumbs

1 egg, beaten

sea salt and freshly ground black pepper

serves 4

Slice the tops and bottoms off of the onions, taking only a little at the root end and more at the top. Scoop out the insides, leaving 2–3 layers of the outer onion as a shell. Put the scooped-out onion flesh in a food processor and process until finely chopped.

Put 1 tablespoon of the oil in a frying pan and add 4 tablespoons of the chopped onions. Cook for 3–5 minutes, until soft. Add the lamb, season well, and cook for 5–7 minutes, stirring to break up the meat. Stir in the garlic, tomato purée, wine, cinnamon, dill and mint and cook for 2–3 minutes, stirring. Taste and adjust the seasoning. Remove from the heat and leave to cool.

Preheat the oven to 200°C (400°F) Gas 6. Add the rice in an even layer in the bottom of the baking dish. Brush the inside of the onion shells with oil and sprinkle with salt.

When the stuffing is cool enough to handle, stir in the breadcrumbs, egg, and 2–3 tablespoons water. The mixture should be soft, but not soupy. Spoon the mixture into the onion shells, filling all the way to the top. Arrange the filled onions on top of the rice and brush the outsides with oil. Pour 500 ml water into the dish.

Bake in the preheated oven for 1–1½ hours, until the rice is cooked. Keep an eye on the rice and begin testing it after 1 hour in the oven. You may need to add more water. Serve immediately or let cool and serve with a mixed green salad on the side.

french onion soup

50 g unsalted butter

1 tablespoon olive oil

3 large onions, about 1.3 kg, thinly sliced

2 garlic cloves, crushed

1 tablespoon plain flour

1 litre beef, chicken or vegetable stock

600 ml dry white wine

1 fresh bay leaf

2 sprigs of fresh thyme

1 baguette, sliced

about 180 g Gruyère cheese, finely grated

coarse sea salt and freshly ground black pepper

serves 4–6

Put the butter and oil in a large saucepan and melt over medium heat. Add the onions and cook over low heat for 15–20 minutes, until soft.

Add the garlic and flour and cook, stirring for about 1 minute. Add the stock, wine, bay leaf and thyme. Season with salt and pepper and bring to the boil. Boil for 1 minute, then lower the heat and simmer very gently for 20 minutes. Taste and adjust the seasoning. At this point, the soup will be cooked, but standing time will improve the flavour – at least 30 minutes.

Before serving, preheat the grill. Put the baguette slices on a baking tray and brown under the grill until lightly toasted. Set aside. Do not turn the grill off.

To serve, ladle the soup into ovenproof bowls and top with a few toasted baguette rounds. Sprinkle grated cheese over the top and cook under the grill until browned and bubbling. Serve immediately.

roasted onions & sausages

3 white or red onions (or a mixture of both), cut into wedges

olive oil, to drizzle

4 eating apples

12 good-quality chipolatas or other sausages

serves 4

Preheat the oven to 200°C (400°F) Gas 6.

Scatter the onions over a heavy-based roasting tin. Drizzle over a little olive oil.

Core the apples and cut them into quarters. Add to the roasting tin, top with the sausages and drizzle with a little more oil. Roast in the preheated oven for about 30 minutes, turning halfway through.

crispy onion rings

two red onions, cut into ½–cm thick rings

two white onions, cut into ½–cm thick rings

250 ml buttermilk

55 g chickpea flour

60 g cornflour

1 teaspoon sea salt

2 eggs

500 ml vegetable oil

serves 4

Put the onion slices in a large bowl and gently toss to separate the rings. Add the buttermilk and stir. Set aside for 1 hour.

Put the chickpea flour, cornflour and salt in a bowl. Make a well in the centre. Use a slotted spoon to remove the onions from the buttermilk (reserving the buttermilk) and transfer them to a colander to drain off any excess liquid. Put 125 ml of the reserved buttermilk in a bowl and beat in the eggs until just combined. Pour this mixture into the flour mixture and beat well to form a smooth, thick batter.

Put the oil in a frying pan set over medium/high heat. Toss a handful of onion rings into the batter and lift them out with a slotted spoon (letting any excess batter drip back into the bowl). Put them in the frying pan. Cook for about 1 minute, or until golden. Remove from the oil with a slotted spoon and drain on kitchen paper. Repeat with the remaining onion rings. Serve warm.

Pictured with Potato & Parsnip Croquettes – recipe on page 11.

braised onions

750 g small onions

4 tablespoons olive oil

4 garlic cloves, peeled and halved lengthways

a sprig of bay leaves

1 teaspoon smoked sweet paprika (pimentón dulce)

4 tablespoons dry white wine

coarse sea salt and freshly ground black pepper

serves 4

Peel the onions, but leave the root end on.

Heat the oil in a heavy or cast iron enamelled heatproof casserole with a lid. Add the onions, garlic and bay leaves and cook over medium heat for 5 minutes. Stir often to stop them browning.

Add the paprika, salt, pepper and wine, cover and cook slowly until just tender, about 25 minutes (however, they can take up to 45 minutes depending on size).

pickled onions

60 g salt

500 g shallots or pickling onions

spiced vinegar

8 mixed peppercorns

4 whole cloves

1-cm cinnamon stick

1-cm piece fresh ginger

400 ml malt vinegar

500-g jar, sterilized (see note on page 4)

makes 500 g

To make a brine, put the salt in a saucepan with 600 ml water. Bring to the boil, remove from the heat and let cool.

Peel the shallots and put them in a bowl, add the cooled brine and leave for 24 hours. After this time, drain, rinse in cold water and dry.

To make the spiced vinegar, put the peppercorns, cloves, cinnamon and ginger in a small saucepan. Add the vinegar, cover and bring to the boil over low heat. Turn off the heat, let cool, then strain.

Pack the onions into the jar, pushing them down with the handle of a wooden spoon. Top up with the cooled spiced vinegar. Tap the sides to remove any air bubbles or slide a thin knife blade down the inside of the jar to release them. Cover with a waxed paper disc or baking paper, seal the jar and store in a cool, dark cupboard until required. Wait at least 3 months before tasting.

fruiting vegetables

baked stuffed aubergines ❧ griddled aubergines with lemon & mint ❧ **aubergine, red pepper & tomato tart** moussaka ❧ **pan-grilled aubergine with honey & spices** fiery red pepper soup ❧ **red pepper scones** three pepper tagine with eggs ❧ **grilled pepper, tomato & chilli salad** ❧ roasted red pepper & walnut dip **smoky pepper & aubergine salsa** ❧ crunchy pepper & sweetcorn relish ❧ **casablancan stuffed tomatoes** slow-cooked tomatoes with goats' cheese & garlic toasts **triple tomato & basil risotto** ❧ roast tomato ketchup **upside-down tomato tart** ❧ tomato soup **tomato, mozzarella & basil salad** ❧ chilli tomato jam **roasted tomatoes** ❧ sweetcorn, asparagus & goats' cheese frittata ❧ **sweetcorn, courgette & cumin soup** ❧ barbecued sweetcorn with chilli lime butter ❧ **sweetcorn & sun-dried tomato corn bread** ❧ tagine of artichokes, potatoes & peas **pan-fried artichokes with thyme & ricotta**

Versatile and filling, aubergines can be used in many ways, and make a great vegetarian alternative. This dish of baked stuffed aubergines can be served as a course on its own or as a side dish to roasted and grilled meats. The harissa (see note on page 59) adds a wonderful touch of warmth. Serve with chunks of crusty bread to mop up the delicious juices.

baked stuffed aubergines

2 aubergines, halved lengthways

2–3 tablespoons olive oil, plus extra for drizzling

1 onion, chopped

2 tomatoes, skinned and chopped plus 1 tomato, skinned and thinly sliced

50 g fresh breadcrumbs, toasted

2 garlic cloves, crushed

a small bunch of fresh coriander, chopped

1–2 teaspoons harissa paste

1 teaspoon sugar

sea salt and freshly ground black pepper

serves 4

Preheat the oven to 180°C (350°F) Gas 4. Using a spoon, scoop out the aubergine flesh and place it on a chopping board. Brush the insides of the empty aubergine shells with a little olive oil, place them on a baking tray and bake them in the oven for 4–5 minutes.

Meanwhile, coarsely chop the aubergine flesh. Heat the remaining oil in a pan and fry the onions to soften. Add the aubergine flesh, cook for a few minutes more then stir in the tomatoes. Add the breadcrumbs, garlic, coriander, harissa and sugar. Season to taste with salt and pepper.

Spoon the mixture into the empty aubergine shells. Arrange the slices of tomato on the top of each one, drizzle with a little olive oil and bake in the preheated oven for 20–25 minutes. Serve hot.

Although simplicity itself to make, the success of this dish relies on griddling the aubergines perfectly. There is nothing worse than undercooked aubergine, so make sure you baste with plenty of oil, and don't let the pan get too hot or the aubergines will burn before they brown – they should gently sizzle. Add a little crushed or chopped garlic to the dressing if you like, but the mint and lemon flavours are quite delicate so show restraint.

griddled aubergines
with lemon & mint

2 medium aubergines (about 500 g)

olive oil, for basting

dressing

100 ml extra virgin olive oil

finely grated zest and freshly squeezed juice of 1 lemon

2 tablespoons balsamic vinegar

1–2 teaspoons sugar

4 tablespoons very coarsely chopped fresh mint

sea salt and freshly ground black pepper

a ridged griddle pan or barbecue

serves 4

To make the dressing, put the oil, lemon zest and juice and balsamic vinegar in a bowl and whisk well. Add the sugar, salt and pepper to taste – it should be fairly sweet. Stir in half the mint, then set aside.

Heat a ridged griddle pan until hot or light a barbecue and wait for the coals to turn white. Cut each aubergine lengthways into 8 thin slices, brush liberally with olive oil, add to the pan or barbecue and cook for 2–3 minutes on each side, until golden brown and lightly charred. Arrange the slices on a large platter and spoon the dressing over the top.

Cover and set aside so that the aubergines absorb the flavours of the dressing. Sprinkle with the remaining chopped mint and serve warm or at room temperature.

This deliciously easy tart is packed full of juicy summer vegetables. It's a great choice for a sophisticated picnic with friends.

aubergine, red pepper & tomato tart

160 g baby aubergine, halved lengthways (or normal aubergine, chopped)

2 large red peppers, deseeded and cut into strips

1 large red onion, thinly sliced

50 ml olive oil, plus extra to drizzle

1 teaspoon salt

½ teaspoon crushed black pepper

100 g cherry tomatoes, halved

1 tablespoon chopped fresh parsley

110 g mature Cheddar, grated

150 g Greek yoghurt

pizza dough base

220 g strong flour

1 teaspoon dried quick yeast

½ teaspoon salt

2 tablespoons olive oil

1 egg

80 ml warm water

a 23-cm loose-based fluted tart tin, greased

makes about 8 slices

Preheat the oven to 180°C (350°F) Gas 4.

Put the aubergine, peppers and onion in a roasting tin (preferably non-stick), drizzle with oil, and season with the salt and pepper. Cover the tray with aluminium foil. Bake in the preheated oven for about 20 minutes, or until just soft. Remove from the oven and leave to cool, then chop the aubergine flesh (if you haven't already done so). Drain any excess juice from the roasted vegetables.

Reduce the oven temperature to 170°C (325°F) Gas 3.

To make the dough base, mix the flour, yeast and salt in a bowl. Make a well in the centre and pour in the oil, egg and water. Draw everything together with your hands until you get a soft dough.

Transfer the dough to a lightly floured surface and knead for a couple of minutes. The dough should be soft but not sticky. If it is sticky, add a little flour and knead again. Roll out the dough with a rolling pin until 3 mm thick.

Line the tart tin with the dough but do not trim the edges yet. Set aside.

Stir the tomatoes, parsley and half the cheese into the roasted vegetables and set aside.

In a separate bowl, mix together the yoghurt and remaining cheese, then spoon into the tart shell.

Scatter the roasted vegetable mixture evenly over the yoghurt. Now trim the excess pizza dough neatly around the edges. Bake in the oven for 25–30 minutes. Remove from the oven and leave to cool.

*tip

Plenty of oil is required when cooking aubergines as it draws the heat inside the vegetable to aid cooking and also keeps it moist. Salting aubergines before you begin cooking with them means that their spongy flesh absorbs less oil and you get a healthier, less greasy result. Dissolve a handful of salt in a bowl of cold water and add the sliced or diced aubergine to it. Set a lid or plate on top to keep them submerged and leave for about an hour to draw out the bitter juices. After this time, tip into a colander, rinse and pat dry with kitchen paper. You can then use the aubergine as directed in the recipe.

Some recipes for traditional Greek moussaka call for potatoes alongside the aubergines, and some have potatoes only. This one is all aubergine. Another departure here is the yoghurt topping in place of the classic béchamel sauce, which makes for a lighter dish. This improves over time so is best made a day in advance, refrigerated and baked when ready to serve. The Moroccan-style pan-grilled aubergine is bursting with hot, spicy, sweet and fruity flavours – simple to prepare, it packs a real flavour-punch.

moussaka

1 onion, chopped

4–5 tablespoons olive oil

500 g lamb mince

2 garlic cloves, finely chopped

½ teaspoon ground allspice

¼ teaspoon ground cinnamon

2 teaspoons dried oregano

125 ml red wine

2 x 400-g tins chopped tomatoes

1 bay leaf, plus extra to garnish

a pinch of sugar

3 medium aubergines, sliced into 1-cm rounds

sea salt and freshly ground black pepper

for the topping

350 ml Greek yoghurt

2 eggs, beaten

150 g feta, crumbled

a large handful of fresh mint leaves, chopped

3 tablespoons freshly grated Parmesan

a 30 x 20 cm baking dish

serves 6

Combine the onion and 1 tablespoon of the oil in a large frying pan. Cook the onion for about 3–5 minutes, until soft. Add the lamb, season well and cook, stirring, for about 5 minutes, until browned. Add the garlic, allspice, cinnamon and oregano and cook for 1 minute. Add the wine and cook for 1 minute more. Add the tomatoes, bay leaf and sugar and mix well. Let simmer gently, uncovered, while you prepare the aubergines.

Preheat the oven to 200°C (400°F) Gas 6.

Heat a few tablespoons of the oil in a large non-stick frying pan. Add the aubergine slices in a single layer and cook to brown slightly. Using tongs, turn and cook the other sides, then transfer to kitchen paper to drain. Work in batches, adding more oil as necessary, until all the aubergine slices are browned.

In a bowl, combine the yoghurt, eggs and feta and mix well with a fork until blended. Season well with salt and pepper and stir in the mint. Set aside.

To assemble the moussaka, arrange half of the lamb mixture on the bottom of the baking dish. Top with half of the aubergine slices. Repeat once more. Spread the yoghurt mixture on top and level the surface. Sprinkle with the Parmesan and decorate with bay leaves. Bake in the preheated oven for about 40–50 minutes, until golden brown and bubbling. Serve immediately.

pan-grilled aubergine with honey & spices

8 aubergines, thickly sliced lengthways

olive oil, for brushing

2–3 cloves garlic, crushed

a thumb-sized piece of fresh ginger, peeled and crushed

1 teaspoon ground cumin

1 teaspoon harissa paste*

5 tablespoons runny honey

freshly squeezed juice of 1 lemon

sea salt

a small bunch of fresh flat leaf parsley, finely chopped

couscous, to serve

4 metal or wooden skewers, to serve (optional)

serves 4

Brush each aubergine slice with olive oil and cook them in a stove-top grill pan or grill them under a conventional grill, turning them over so that they are lightly browned.

In a wok or large heavy frying pan, fry the garlic in a little olive oil, then stir in the ginger, cumin, harissa, honey and lemon juice. Add a little water to thin it, then place the aubergine slices in the liquid and cook gently for about 10 minutes, until they have absorbed the sauce. Add more water if necessary and season to taste with salt.

Thread the aubergines onto the skewers, if using, and garnish with the parsley. Serve hot or at room temperature as meal on their own with couscous, or as an accompaniment to grilled meat.

*Note Harissa is a fiercely hot red chilli purée from North Africa, where it is used extensively as a condiment and diluted with stock, water or fresh tomato sauce to flavour couscous dishes, soups and tagines (stews).

This fiery soup will add heat to your belly on a cold day! But if you are making it for children, omit the chillies and use 500 ml milk mixed with 500 ml stock. The perfect accompaniment to the soup is these delicious red pepper scones. The secret with scones is just to make them nice and thick. Serve these warm with butter – they are irresistible.

fiery red pepper soup

6 medium red peppers

375 g carrots

1–2 fresh red chillies

750 g ripe plum tomatoes

3 large garlic cloves, peeled

6 tablespoons olive oil

2 teaspoons smoked sweet paprika (pimentón dulce)

1.2 litres vegetable or beef stock

sea salt and freshly ground black pepper

crisply fried bacon slices, to serve

serves 8

Preheat the oven to 200°C (400°F) Gas 6.

Cut the stalk ends off the peppers, halve and scrape out the seeds. Scrape the carrots and cut into chunky fingers.

If using chillies, cut off the stalks, cut in half and scrape out the seeds (using rubber gloves if you like).

Put the peppers, carrots, chillies, tomatoes and garlic in large roasting tins so the vegetables aren't too cramped, then toss them in the olive oil. Season well with salt and pepper and roast in the preheated oven for about 30 minutes, until all the vegetables are soft and slightly charred at the edges.

Transfer half the vegetables to a blender, add the paprika and half the stock and blend until smooth. Pour into a saucepan and repeat with the remaining vegetables and stock, adding extra stock if it seems too thick. Reheat until almost boiling, add salt and pepper to taste, then serve with the bacon crumbled over the top.

red pepper scones

225 g self-raising flour

50 g butter, diced

1 teaspoon baking powder

1 tablespoon freshly chopped rosemary, plus 10 small sprigs

100 g roasted red peppers, drained and finely chopped

1 egg

50 ml milk, plus extra to glaze

makes 10–12

Preheat the oven to 220°C (425°F) Gas 7.

Mix the flour and butter in a food processor or with your fingertips until it resembles crumbs. Mix in the baking powder, chopped rosemary, a pinch of salt and the peppers. Beat the egg with the milk, then pour into the flour, stirring with a knife until you have a smooth dough. Roll out the dough on a lightly floured surface so it is at least 2 cm thick and cut out 5-cm circles. Keep rerolling until you have 10–12 scones. Push the rosemary sprigs into the tops, place on a baking tray, brush with milk and bake for 15 minutes until golden.

Juicy, sweet, sun-ripened peppers feature heavily in the cuisine of Morocco. The gentle aromatic spicing of this cooked salad is just perfect for a warm summer evening. The tagine is one of those dishes you'll find in Morocco at street stalls, bus stations and working men's cafes. Quick, easy and colourful, it is a great dish for lunch or a tasty snack. Serve either dish with warmed flat breads or pita bread.

three pepper tagine with eggs

2 tablespoons olive oil or ghee

1 onion, halved lengthways and sliced

2–3 garlic cloves, chopped

1–2 teaspoons coriander seeds

1 teaspoon cumin seeds

3 peppers (green, red and yellow), deseeded and cut into slices

2 tablespoons green olives, stoned and finely sliced

sea salt and freshly ground black pepper

4–6 very fresh eggs

1 teaspoon paprika or dried red chilli flakes

leaves from a small bunch of fresh flat leaf parsley, coarsely chopped

warmed flatbreads, to serve

serves 4–6

Heat the olive oil in the base of a tagine, flameproof baking dish or heavy-based frying pan. Add the onions, garlic, coriander and cumin seeds and sauté, stirring, until the onions begin to soften. Toss in the peppers and olives and sauté until they begin to colour. Season well with salt and pepper.

Using your spoon, push aside the peppers to form little pockets for the eggs. Crack the eggs in the pockets and cover for 4–5 minutes until the eggs are cooked. Scatter the paprika over the top and sprinkle with the parsley. Serve immediately from the tagine or pan, with warmed flatbread on the side.

grilled pepper, tomato & chilli salad

2 green peppers

3–4 Marmara or other long sweet peppers

400 g ripe tomatoes, skinned (see note on page 69)

¼ teaspoon smoked sweet paprika (pimentón dulce)

¼ teaspoon ground cumin

1 tablespoon freshly squeezed lemon juice

2 tablespoons olive oil

20 g pickled sliced Jalapeño chillies, rinsed and finely chopped

1 heaped tablespoon finely chopped parsley

sea salt and freshly ground black pepper

serves 6

To skin the green and sweet peppers, either lay them over a low gas flame, turning frequently until the skins char, or halve them, lay them skin-side upwards on a grill pan and grill under high heat until the skins are blackened. Put the charred peppers in a bowl and cover with clingfilm (the trapped steam helps to loosen the skins). Once the peppers are cool, the skins should peel off easily.

Deseed the peppers, slice them thickly and put in a serving bowl with the tomatoes. Measure the paprika and cumin into another small bowl and whisk in the lemon juice and oil. Season to taste with salt and pepper. Pour the dressing over the peppers, add the Jalapeños and parsley and toss together.

This is a traditional Syrian dip called muhammara. There it would be served as part of a meze selection, with hoummus, aubergine dip (baba ganoush), olives, pickles, cheese and flatbreads. It also works well as a spooning sauce to serve with baked or grilled fish or lamb. It's perfect for entertaining as it benefits from being made a day in advance.

roasted red pepper & walnut dip

Cook the peppers one at a time by skewering each one on a fork and holding it directly over a gas flame for 10–15 minutes, until the skin is blackened all over. Alternatively, put them on a baking tray and then in an oven preheated to 220ºC (425ºF) Gas 7. Cook them for about 10–15 minutes, until the skin has puffed up and blackened all over. Transfer to a bowl, cover with a tea towel and leave until cool enough to handle.

Using your hands, remove the skin and seeds from the peppers and tear the flesh into pieces. (Avoid rinsing with water, as this will remove the smoky flavour.) Put it in a food processor and add the remaining ingredients. Process to a coarse paste. Season to taste with salt and pepper and transfer to a bowl. Cover with clingfilm and refrigerate for 8 hours or ideally overnight to allow the flavours to fully develop.

To serve, bring the dip to room temperature and transfer it to a shallow bowl. Drizzle with olive oil and sprinkle with chopped pistachios. Serve with torn toasted flatbreads. It will keep in an airtight container in the refrigerator for 4–5 days.

3 large red peppers

1 slice of day-old sourdough bread, cut into small pieces

100 g walnut halves, coarsely chopped

½ teaspoon dried chilli flakes

1 tablespoon sun-dried tomato paste

2 garlic cloves, chopped

2 teaspoons freshly squeezed lemon juice

1 tablespoon balsamic vinegar

2 teaspoons caster sugar

1 teaspoon ground cumin

2 tablespoons olive oil, plus extra to serve

chopped pistachios, to sprinkle

sea salt and freshly ground black pepper

toasted flatbread, roughly torn, to serve

serves 6–8

Sweet red peppers form a great base for condiments to serve with all types of food. This smoky-flavoured pepper and aubergine salsa is great with barbecued food, especially as a flavour-boost on burgers and sausages. Fresh sweetcorn and colourful peppers make a vibrant relish and the crunchy texture also adds appeal. You can serve the relish the day you make it, but it's even better preserved.

smoky pepper & aubergine salsa

2 red peppers
1 aubergine
3 tablespoons olive oil
1 red onion, finely chopped
3 garlic cloves, chopped
1–2 teaspoons minced red chilli
1 teaspoon sugar
½ teaspoon sea salt

1 tablespoon freshly squeezed lemon juice
a small bunch of fresh flat leaf parsley, chopped
2 tablespoons freshly chopped dill
2 teaspoons ground sumac*

makes about 625 ml

Roast the aubergine and red peppers directly over the flame of a gas burner or barbecue, or put under a preheated grill, turning regularly, until completely blackened and soft. Put them in a large bowl, cover with a lid or clingfilm and let them steam for 10 minutes. Remove and peel off all the blackened skin and discard. Remove the stems and seeds from the peppers and chop the flesh very finely. Cut the stem off the aubergine and chop the flesh very finely.

Heat 1 tablespoon of the oil in a frying pan, add the onion and garlic and sauté for 5 minutes until soft. Transfer to a large bowl with the peppers, aubergine, remaining oil, chilli, sugar, salt, lemon juice, parsley and dill and mix well. Place in a serving bowl and sprinkle with the sumac. The salsa will keep in the refrigerator for 3 days.

*Note Sumac is a spice widely used in Turkish, Lebanese and Iranian cooking. The red berries have an astringent quality with a pleasing sour-fruit flavour. They are used whole, but ground sumac is available from Middle Eastern grocers or specialist online retailers.

crunchy pepper & sweetcorn relish

3 peppers (1 red, 1 yellow and 1 orange)
sweetcorn kernels from 2 corn-on-the-cobs
1 red or white onion, chopped
4 tablespoons sea salt
1 teaspoon white mustard seeds
½ teaspoon cumin seeds

½ teaspoon coriander seeds
½ teaspoon whole black peppercorns
6 small dried chillies
375 ml white (distilled) vinegar
115 g sugar
¼ teaspoon ground turmeric

makes about 900 ml

Remove the stems from the peppers and discard. Cut the peppers into 2-cm dice and put in a colander with the sweetcorn and onion. Toss with the salt and leave for 2–4 hours. Rinse well with cold water and shake dry.

Heat a saucepan over medium heat and add the mustard, cumin and coriander seeds, peppercorns and chillies. Cook, stirring, for 1 minute until fragrant. Add the vinegar, sugar and turmeric and bring to the boil, stirring to dissolve the sugar.

Add the rinsed sweetcorn, peppers and onion to the vinegar mixture. Cover and bring to the boil.

If using immediately, let cool, stirring occasionally. To preserve, fill sterilized jars with the relish while it is still hot and seal (see note on page 4). The relish will keep for up to 2 months if sealed correctly.

casablancan stuffed tomatoes

150 g couscous
½ teaspoon salt
150 ml warm water
3–4 tablespoons olive oil, plus extra for drizzling
4 large tomatoes
1 onion, finely chopped
1 carrot, peeled and diced
a sprinkling of sugar

1–2 teaspoons ras-el-hanout
a bunch each of fresh flat leaf parsley and coriander, finely chopped
½ preserved lemon, finely chopped
sea salt and freshly ground black pepper

serves 4

Preheat the oven to 180°C (350°F) Gas 4.

Put the couscous in a bowl. Stir the salt into the warm water and pour it over the couscous, stirring all the time so that the water is absorbed evenly. Leave the couscous to swell for about 10 minutes before using your fingers to rub 1 tablespoon of the oil into the couscous grains to break up the lumps and aerate them.

Slice the top off each tomato and set aside. Using a spoon, scoop out the pulp and seeds and reserve in a bowl. In a heavy-based saucepan, heat the remaining olive oil and stir in the onion and carrot. Fry until they begin to caramelize, then stir in the tomato pulp and sugar. Add the ras-el-hanout and cook until the mixture forms a thick sauce. Season to taste with salt and pepper.

Tip the spicy tomato mixture onto the couscous and mix well. Add the fresh herbs and preserved lemon and toss until it is thoroughly combined. Spoon the couscous into each tomato cavity and place a top on each one like a lid. Put the filled tomatoes in a baking dish, drizzle with a little olive oil and bake in the preheated oven for about 25 minutes. Serve hot or leave to cool and eat at room temperature.

Nothing sings of summer quite like ripe, juicy tomatoes, baked until they become sweet. In Casablanca, these tomatoes stuffed with couscous and herbs are popular as a starter, or they are served on their own with a salad. For both recipes here, it's crucial to use super-ripe tomatoes.

slow-cooked tomatoes with goats' cheese & garlic toasts

500 ml extra virgin olive oil
1 sprig of fresh oregano
2 teaspoons finely chopped fresh flat leaf parsley leaves
6 very ripe Roma tomatoes
½ teaspoon sea salt

200 g soft goats' cheese
1 small baguette
2 garlic cloves, peeled

serves 4

Preheat the oven to 130°C (250°F) Gas ½.

Put the oil in a small, non-reactive baking dish. Add the oregano and parsley. Cut the tomatoes in half and arrange them in a single layer in the dish. Ideally you want the tomatoes to be almost fully submerged in the oil. Sprinkle the salt evenly over the tomatoes. Cook in the preheated oven for about 5 hours, until the tomatoes are intensely red and softened yet still retain their shape. Remove from the oven and leave the tomatoes in the oil to cool completely.

Put the goats' cheese in a serving bowl.

Preheat the grill. Slice the baguette very thinly. Toast the bread on both sides until golden and crisp and rub one side with the peeled garlic cloves.

Remove the tomatoes from the oil and arrange them on a serving platter with the goats' cheese and garlic toasts on the side.

triple tomato & basil risotto

400 g whole baby plum tomatoes

4 tablespoons olive oil

about 1 litre hot vegetable stock

500 ml passata (Italian puréed, sieved tomatoes)

125 g unsalted butter

1 onion, finely chopped

8 pieces sun-dried or mi-cuit tomatoes (not the ones in oil), chopped

400 g risotto rice, preferably vialone nano

150 ml light red wine

50 g freshly grated Parmesan cheese

4 tablespoons chopped fresh basil

sea salt and freshly ground black pepper

extra basil leaves, to serve

freshly grated Parmesan cheese, to serve

serves 4

Put the plum tomatoes in a roasting tin and pour over the olive oil. Mix them well to coat and season with salt and pepper. Roast in a preheated oven at 200°C (400°F) Gas 6 for about 20 minutes or until they are slightly collapsed and the skins beginning to brown. Remove from the oven and set aside.

Pour the stock and passata into a saucepan, stir well, then heat to a gentle simmer. Melt half the butter in a large, heavy saucepan and add the onion and chopped sun-dried tomatoes. Cook gently for 10 minutes until soft, golden and translucent but not browned. Add the rice and stir until well coated with the butter and heated through. Pour in the wine and boil hard until it has reduced and almost disappeared. This will remove the taste of raw alcohol. Remove from the heat.

Return the risotto to the heat, warm through, then begin adding the stock, a large ladle at a time, stirring gently until each ladle has almost been absorbed by the rice. The risotto should be kept at a bare simmer throughout cooking, so don't let the rice dry out – add more stock as necessary. Continue until the rice is tender and creamy, but the grains still firm (15–20 minutes depending on the type of rice used – check the packet instructions).

Season to taste with salt and pepper, beat in the remaining butter, the Parmesan and chopped basil. You may like to add a little more hot stock at this stage to loosen the risotto – it should be quite wet. Cover and let rest for a couple of minutes so the risotto can relax and the cheese melt. Carefully ladle into warm bowls and cover the surface with the roasted tomatoes and any juices. Add the basil leaves and serve immediately with extra grated Parmesan cheese.

Tomato and rice soup at its best! This risotto is full of the intense flavour of tomatoes, added in three ways: passata to the stock; sun-dried tomatoes adding their caramel flavour deep in the risotto; then tiny ripe plum tomatoes, roasted to perfect sweetness. Delicious hot – but any leftovers are irresistible and so marvellous eaten straight out of the pan too.

✳ tip

If a recipe requires you to skin tomatoes, make a small cut near the stalk of each one with a sharp knife, put them in a heatproof bowl and pour over boiling water. Leave for a minute, then pour the water away and cover the tomatoes with cold water. The skins should now peel off easily.

roast tomato ketchup

2 kg tomatoes

3 teaspoons sea salt

leaves from a small bunch
of fresh thyme

2 tablespoons olive oil

1 white onion, chopped

1 teaspoon allspice berries

½ teaspoon whole cloves

½ teaspoon black peppercorns

400 g sugar

1 teaspoon dry mustard
powder

500 ml cider vinegar

makes about 1.5 litres

Preheat the oven to 150°C (300°F) Gas 2.

Cut the tomatoes in half and arrange cut-side up in a roasting tin.
Sprinkle with 2 teaspoons of the salt and all the thyme leaves and
drizzle with 1 tablespoon of the oil. Roast in the preheated oven
for 1½ hours.

Heat the remaining 1 tablespoon of oil in a large saucepan over
medium heat, add the onion and sauté for 10 minutes until golden.

Put the allspice, cloves and peppercorns in a mortar and pestle and
grind to a powder. Add to the onion and cook for 1 minute. Add the
roasted tomatoes, sugar, mustard powder, vinegar and remaining
1 teaspoon salt and bring to the boil. Adjust the heat to a steady
low boil and cook for 30 minutes, uncovered, stirring occasionally.

Blend to a thick sauce using a food processor or handheld blender.
Pour into sterilized bottles and seal (see note on page 4).

The ketchup will keep for up to 1 year if properly sealed and stored
in a cool, dark place.

Fresh, homemade tomato ketchup is vastly superior
to store-bought varieties as it manages to capture
the true flavour of tomatoes in season. This recipe
calls for the tomatoes to be slow-roasted as this
results in a more intense flavour, but one that is
not as full-on as barbecue sauce. The sweetness of
summer-ripe tomatoes is also perfectly captured in
this tart, which is essentially a tomato tarte tatin.
It is flavoured with fresh rosemary and little capers,
but you could add any combination of ingredients
that takes your fancy, such as Ligurian olives, garlic,
oregano or anchovies.

upside-down tomato tart

2 tablespoons light olive oil

2 teaspoons small capers,
rinsed if salted

10–12 fresh rosemary needles

3 ripe tomatoes, thickly sliced

375-g sheet ready-rolled puff
pastry, defrosted if frozen

cracked black pepper

extra virgin olive oil, for
drizzling

*a non-stick, heatproof frying
pan 20–23 cm diameter*

serves 4, as a starter

Preheat the oven to 220°C (425°F) Gas 7.

Put the oil, capers and rosemary in a heatproof non-stick frying pan.
Put over high heat and when the capers start to sizzle add the
tomatoes, firmly pressing them down in a single layer in the pan.
Cook for 3–4 minutes to allow the tomatoes to sizzle and soften.

Place the sheet of pastry over the tomatoes, folding in the corners,
being careful not to press down on the tomatoes. Transfer the pan
to the preheated oven and cook for 18–20 minutes, until the pastry
is puffed and golden. Remove the pan from the oven and let the tart
rest for a couple of minutes.

Place a serving plate that is larger than the frying pan upside-down
on top of the pan and quickly flip the pan over so the tart falls onto
the plate. Sprinkle with cracked black pepper and a drizzle of olive
oil and cut into 4 wedges to serve.

tomato soup

1 tablespoon olive oil

a knob of butter

1 onion, peeled and finely chopped

1 garlic glove, finely chopped

12 ripe tomatoes, halved

750 ml vegetable stock

a pinch of light soft brown sugar

freshly ground black pepper

a little double cream (optional)

serves 4

Heat the oil and butter in a saucepan, then fry the onion and garlic until softened, but not too brown. When the onion is soft, add the tomatoes and simmer gently, stirring occasionally until the tomatoes have turned to mush and most of the liquid has evaporated, about 20 minutes.

Add the stock, bring to the boil, reduce the heat and simmer gently for 15 minutes.

Purée the soup with a handheld blender or in a food processor. Return to the pan, warm through and add the sugar and pepper. If you want to make this soup really creamy, add a little cream.

tomato, mozzarella & basil salad

2 balls of buffalo mozzarella, 150 g each

2 large ripe tomatoes, roughly the same size as the balls of mozzarella

50 g fresh basil leaves

about 100 ml extra virgin olive oil

sea salt and freshly ground black pepper

serves 4

Cut the mozzarella and tomatoes into slices about 5 mm thick. Arrange the tomato slices on a large plate and season. Put 1 slice of mozzarella on each slice of tomato and top with a basil leaf. Tear up the remaining basil and scatter over the top. Drizzle with a generous amount of olive oil just before serving. Serve immediately at room temperature.

chilli tomato jam

500 g ripe tomatoes, roughly chopped

4 red bird's-eye chillies, roughly chopped

2 garlic cloves, peeled

1 teaspoon grated fresh ginger

2 tablespoons light soy sauce

200 g grated palm sugar

75 ml of white wine vinegar

½ teaspoon of sea salt

makes 300 ml

Put the tomatoes, chillies and garlic in a food processor and process until quite smooth. Transfer to a saucepan and add the remaining ingredients. Bring to the boil and simmer gently, stirring occasionally, for 30–40 minutes, or until thick and jam-like.

Spoon into a sterilized bottle or jar (see page 4) and leave to cool, then seal. Refrigerate once opened.

roasted tomatoes

500 g ripe cherry tomatoes

olive oil, for drizzling

2 garlic cloves, unpeeled

a sprig of fresh rosemary

serves 4

Preheat the oven to 180°C (350°F) Gas 4.

Put the tomatoes into a roasting tin. Drizzle over a little olive oil and the garlic and rosemary. Roast in the preheated oven for 35 minutes. When they are ready to come out of the oven they look wrinkled.

The frittata is a brilliant stand-by for a no-fuss, fast supper. Crunchy sweetcorn and asparagus work nicely here combined with farm-fresh eggs, creamy goats' cheese and fresh, tangy dill. The soup is inspired by the cuisine of America's South-west. The chilli content is rather conservative, but you can spice it up as much as you like. You can also purée it for a thicker, more chowder-like consistency.

sweetcorn, asparagus & goats' cheese frittata

2 bunches of thin asparagus spears

50 g butter

2 corn-on-the-cobs, freshly shucked

4 spring onions, finely chopped

a handful of fresh dill, chopped

8 eggs, beaten

200 g firm goats' cheese, broken into pieces

sea salt and freshly ground black pepper

serves 4

Trim, or snap off, the woody ends from the asparagus and cut the spears into 2–3-cm pieces.

Heat half of the butter in a large non-stick frying pan set over medium heat. Add the asparagus, sweetcorn and spring onions and fry for 2–3 minutes, stirring often. Transfer the vegetables to a large bowl and add the dill, reserving a little to use as garnish. Wipe the pan clean. Add the beaten eggs to the vegetables, gently stirring to combine, and season well with salt and pepper.

Preheat the grill to high. Put the remaining butter in the pan and set over high heat. Swirl the pan around as the butter melts so that it coats the bottom and just starts to sizzle. Pour the frittata mixture into the pan and reduce the heat to medium. Arrange the pieces of goats' cheese over the top of the frittata and gently push them into the mixture. Cook for about 8 minutes, until the sides of the frittata start to puff up (reduce the heat if the bottom appears to be cooking too quickly).

Keep the frittata in the pan and place it under the preheated grill. Cook for 1 minute only just to set the top. Let cool a little in the pan, sprinkle with the reserved dill and serve immediately.

sweetcorn, courgette & cumin soup

3 tablespoons extra virgin olive oil

2 onions, halved, then sliced

3 courgettes, about 600 g, quartered lengthways, then sliced

2–3 potatoes, about 300 g, diced

4 garlic cloves, sliced

2 corn-on-the-cobs, freshly shucked

1 teaspoon ground cumin

1 red chilli, deseeded and sliced

1 litre fresh unsalted chicken or vegetable stock

sea salt

to serve

crème fraîche or cream

chopped fresh coriander

Tabasco sauce

serves 4

Heat the oil in a saucepan. Add the onions, courgettes, potatoes and some salt and cook over high heat until beginning to brown, about 5 minutes.

Add the garlic, sweetcorn, cumin and chilli and cook, stirring, for 1 minute more. Add the stock and 250 ml water, then add salt to taste. Bring to the boil, then lower the heat and simmer gently until the potatoes are tender, 15–20 minutes. Set aside for at least 30 minutes for the flavours to develop.

To serve, reheat the soup. Ladle into soup bowls and top each with a spoonful of crème fraîche, coriander and a dash of Tabasco. Serve immediately.

Note For a light meal, put some flour tortillas on a baking tray, top with grated Cheddar and toast in a hot oven until melted. Cut into wedges to serve.

barbecued sweetcorn with chilli lime butter

12 corn-on-the-cobs, husked
125 g unsalted butter, melted
a large pinch of chilli powder
sea salt and freshly ground black pepper

chilli lime butter

1 teaspoon sweet chilli sauce
finely grated zest and freshly squeezed juice of 2 unwaxed limes
125 g unsalted butter, softened

serves 6

To make the chilli lime butter, put the chilli, lime zest and butter in a bowl and beat well. Season with salt and pepper, then roll into a cylinder between sheets of damp baking paper. Twist the ends and chill for at least 1 hour until hard.

To barbecue the sweetcorn, melt the butter in a small saucepan and whisk in the chilli and lime juice. This will be the basting sauce for the sweetcorn.

Preheat a barbecue or grill, add the sweetcorn and cook for at least 10 minutes, basting and turning until golden brown all over, soft and lightly charred. Slice the chilled butter into disks and serve with the hot grilled corn.

Messy and meltingly delicious, grilled sweetcorn will be a favourite with a hungry crowd. Serve with lots of paper napkins – this is definitely a hands-on dish! And if you have the barbecue already lit, cornbread is a perfect side dish to grilled food. As it doesn't involve yeast, cornbread is a wonderfully easy bread to make at home, ideal to whip up when you want fresh bread, hot from the oven. It is best made in a heavy, cast-iron cooking dish, a skillet or a cast-iron frying pan to achieve a crisp outer crust.

sweetcorn & sun-dried tomato corn bread

2 tablespoons olive oil
175 g coarse yellow cornmeal or instant polenta
125 g plain flour
1 teaspoon baking powder
1 tablespoon rosemary needles
½ teaspoon sea salt
1 egg
250 ml buttermilk

250 ml milk
150 g sweetcorn kernels, fresh or tinned
80 g sun-dried tomatoes, chopped

a heavy baking dish, 28 cm diameter, preferably cast-iron

serves 6

Preheat the oven to 200°C (400°F) Gas 6.

Coat the bottom and sides of the baking dish with the oil. Put in the preheated oven to heat up for 5 minutes.

Combine the cornmeal, flour, baking powder, rosemary and salt in a bowl. Beat together the egg, buttermilk and milk, then carefully fold it into the flour mixture along with the sweetcorn kernels and sun-dried tomatoes.

Remove the baking dish from the oven and pour in the batter. Bake for 30 minutes until set and golden. Let cool on a wire rack.

Slice into wedges to serve. The bread is best eaten while still warm.

You can make this hearty country tagine with fresh or tinned artichokes. If using fresh, see the tip box below on preparing them before you start. Baby artichokes are quite different from the fat, globe ones. They are slightly smaller than the size of your hand, elongated, purple-green and usually sold in bunches. They have very immature chokes inside, which can be eaten. Try them simply pan-fried and paired with delicious cool ricotta and thyme sauce.

tagine of artichokes, potatoes & peas

2–3 tablespoons olive oil

2 red onions, halved lengthways, cut in half crossways, and sliced with the grain

4 garlic cloves, crushed

2 teaspoons coriander seeds

1 teaspoon cumin seeds

2 teaspoons ground turmeric

1–2 teaspoons dried mint

8 medium waxy potatoes, peeled and quartered

350 ml vegetable stock

4 prepared artichokes, quartered

leaves from a small bunch of fresh coriander, chopped

225 g shelled fresh peas or frozen peas

½ preserved lemon, finely shredded

sea salt and freshly ground black pepper

leaves from a small bunch of fresh mint, to serve

crusty bread or couscous, to serve

serves 4–6

Heat the olive oil in a tagine or heavy-based casserole. Add the onion and sauté, stirring, until it begins to soften. Add the garlic, coriander and cumin seeds, ground turmeric and the dried mint. Toss in the potatoes, coating them in the spices. Pour in the stock and bring to the boil. Reduce the heat, cover and cook gently for about 10 minutes.

Toss in the artichokes and fresh coriander and cook for a further 5 minutes. Stir in the peas and preserved lemon, and season to taste with salt and pepper. Cook gently for 5–10 minutes, uncovered, until the artichokes are tender and the liquid has reduced.

Sprinkle with mint leaves and serve with crusty bread or couscous.

✳ tip

To prepare artichokes, you must first remove the outer leaves, then cut off the stems and scoop out the choke and hairy bits with a teaspoon. Rub the artichokes with lemon juice or place in a bowl of cold water with lemon juice to prevent discoloration.

pan-fried artichokes with thyme & ricotta

8–12 medium purple-green young artichokes with stems and heads, about 10 cm long, or 12 whole char-grilled deli artichokes in oil, drained

1½ lemons

100 ml good olive oil

1–2 tablespoons freshly chopped thyme

150 ml dry white wine

at least 125 g fresh ricotta cheese

sea salt and freshly ground black pepper

serves 4

To prepare the artichokes, fill a large bowl with water and squeeze in the juice of ½ lemon. Use another ½ lemon to rub the cut portions of the artichoke as you work. Snap off the dark outer leaves, starting at the base. Trim the stalk down to about 5 cm. Trim away the dark green outer layer at the base and peel the fibrous outside of the stalk with a vegetable peeler. Cut about 1 cm off the tip of each artichoke. As they are prepared, put the artichokes in the lemony water until needed. When ready to cook, drain and cut in half lengthways.

Heat the oil in a large frying pan until hot, then add the artichokes. Fry for 3 minutes without moving them, then turn them over and cook for another 2–3 minutes until tender. If using shop-bought char-grilled artichokes, cut them in half and reheat gently in the olive oil for 3–4 minutes. Transfer to a warm serving dish.

Add the thyme to the frying pan and cook over high heat for a few seconds to release the aroma. Add the wine and boil hard to reduce by half. Season with a squeeze of lemon juice, salt and pepper. Crumble the ricotta around the edge of the plate, pour the hot thyme sauce on top and serve immediately.

podding vegetables

spring vegetable pasta with lemon

pea & mint soup 🌿 **pea & parma ham crostini**

fresh pea, tomato & paneer curry

green couscous with a spring broth

french bean, pea & new potato salad

broad bean, courgette & lemon soup

bean & chickpea salad

green beans with a spanish dressing

florentine green beans 🌿 **french beans with garlic**

This pasta dish is admittedly more vegetable than pasta, but it's one of the most delicious ways to enjoy the new season's produce. You can vary the vegetables depending on what's available. Baby courgettes also work well, as does fennel. The key thing is to cook them until they're only just done to preserve their delicate flavour and bright green colour. Pea soup is another great way to enjoy sweet spring peas – and teamed with mint it is a classic combination.

spring vegetable pasta with lemon

a small bunch of asparagus

150 g shelled fresh peas

a few stalks of sprouting broccoli

150 g shelled broad beans

110 g butter

1 leek or ½ bunch of spring onions, thinly sliced

284-ml carton double cream

300 g dried egg pasta shapes, such as Campanelle

freshly squeezed juice of 2–3 lemons (about 125 ml)

3 heaped tablespoons finely chopped fresh parsley

2 heaped tablespoons each finely chopped fresh dill and chives

sea salt and freshly ground black pepper

freshly shaved Parmesan cheese or grana padano, to serve

serves 6

Snap the asparagus spears two-thirds down the stalks and discard the woody ends. Cut the remaining stem into short lengths. Steam or microwave them for about 2–3 minutes until just cooked and refresh with cold water. Repeat with the other vegetables – steaming them individually until just cooked. (Pop the broad beans out of their skins for an even sweeter taste).

Gently melt the butter in a large saucepan or flameproof casserole and cook the leek for a couple of minutes until starting to soften. Tip in the other vegetables, lightly toss with the butter, cover the pan and leave over very low heat, adding the cream once the vegetables have heated through.

Cook the pasta following the instructions on the packet. Reserve a little of the cooking water and drain well. Tip the drained pasta into the vegetables and toss together. Add the lemon juice and herbs, season with salt and pepper and toss together lightly. Check the seasoning, adding extra salt, pepper, lemon juice or a little of the reserved pasta cooking water to lighten the sauce if you think it needs it. Serve in warm bowls with shavings of Parmesan.

pea & mint soup

50 g butter

2 leeks, trimmed, split, well washed, then chopped

200 g baking potatoes, chopped

1 garlic clove, crushed

750 g frozen peas

1 litre chicken or vegetable stock

2 sprigs of fresh mint

2 tablespoons freshly chopped mint

sea salt and freshly ground black pepper

crème fraîche, to serve

serves 6

Melt the butter in a saucepan, add the leeks, potatoes and garlic and fry for 10 minutes. Add the peas, stock, mint sprigs and a little salt and pepper and bring to the boil. Cover and simmer for 20 minutes. Discard the mint sprigs.

Transfer the soup to a blender, add the chopped mint, then purée until very smooth. Return to the pan, season to taste and heat through. Serve the soup topped with a spoonful of crème fraîche and a generous grinding of black pepper.

* tip

If you have a bumper crop of peas which you are not using straight away, remove them from their pods and freeze them until they are needed. After picking, the sugar in the peas turns to starch very quickly, which impairs their sweet flavour – freezing prevents this. To bring out the sweetness in the peas, add a pinch of sugar to the pan when boiling. Never add salt, as this will make them tough.

pea & parma ham crostini

ciabatta toasts

1 ready-to-bake ciabatta loaf

olive oil spray or 4–6 tablespoons light olive oil

topping

250 g shelled fresh or frozen peas

2 spring onions

40 g finely grated aged pecorino or Parmesan cheese

1 tablespoon finely chopped fresh mint or dill

2 tablespoons fruity olive oil

125 g thinly sliced Parma ham or other air-dried ham, torn or cut in half

salt and freshly ground black pepper

freshly squeezed lemon juice, to taste

makes 18 crostini

To make the ciabatta toasts, preheat the oven to 180°C (350°F) Gas 4. Cut the ciabatta on the slant into fairly thin slices. Spray both sides with olive oil or pour olive oil in the baking trays and dip the slices of ciabatta in it. Bake for 15 minutes, turning the slices halfway through. Remove from the oven and let cool.

For the topping, cook the peas in boiling water for 2–3 minutes or until just tender. Drain under cold running water. Trim and cut the spring onions in half lengthways, then slice very thinly.

Put the peas and onions in a food processor and pulse until you get a chunky spread. Add the pecorino and mint and pulse again, then stir in the olive oil. Season to taste with salt, pepper and lemon juice. Spread the mixture thickly on ciabatta toasts and drape with a piece of ham. Serve immediately.

The new season's peas are so deliciously sweet that you want to enjoy them every which way you can. Teamed with Italian cheese and ham, puréed peas make a wonderful topping for little crostini to be served with drinks. For something more substantial, this fresh-tasting, summery curry is sure to delight guests. Southern Indian food tends to have a greater emphasis on fresh ingredients, with just one or two spices thrown in. Paneer is a firm, white cheese from India – if you can't find it, halloumi works well too.

fresh pea, tomato & paneer curry

2 tablespoons vegetable oil

250 g paneer, cubed

1 tablespoon butter

2 onions, finely chopped

5-cm piece of fresh ginger, grated

2 green chillies, deseeded and finely chopped

3 ripe tomatoes, roughly chopped

2 teaspoons white wine vinegar

200 g fresh peas, shelled, or frozen peas

½ teaspoon garam masala

a handful of fresh coriander leaves

sea salt and freshly ground black pepper

to serve

cooked basmati rice

naan bread

mango chutney

serves 4

Heat the oil in a frying pan set over medium heat. Add the paneer and cook for 4–5 minutes, turning often, until golden all over. Remove from the pan and set aside.

Add the butter to the pan. When it is melted and sizzling, add the onions and stir-fry until softened and lightly golden. Add the ginger and chillies to the pan and cook for 1 minute.

Add the tomatoes, vinegar and 65 ml water and bring to the boil. Cook for about 5 minutes, to thicken slightly. Add the peas and return the paneer to the pan. Reduce the heat and simmer for about 4–5 minutes, until the peas are tender.

Stir in the garam masala and season to taste with salt and pepper. Sprinkle with the coriander leaves and serve with basmati rice and an assortment of Indian accompaniments.

These three recipes are very useful for using up produce from the allotment. The vegetables featured are very easy to grow and tend to produce high yields. Green couscous is a fresh-tasting, summery dish, inspired by the cuisine of Morocco. The salad is so simple that the flavours of the vegetables really shine through, although you could try adding tinned tuna, olives and tomatoes to it to make it more like a French salade Niçoise. Likewise, adding a scoop of risotto rice to this delicious lemon-scented soup (along with a little extra stock to compensate) can turn a light lunch into a hearty meal. If you are using large beans for the soup you might want to slip them out of their pale green jackets, but this is a real labour of love!

green couscous with a spring broth

500 g couscous

½ teaspoon sea salt

600 ml warm water

1–2 tablespoons olive oil

15 g butter, broken into small pieces

1 litre vegetable or chicken stock

350 g fresh broad beans, shelled

200 g fresh or frozen peas

12 spring onions, trimmed and thickly sliced

6 baby courgettes, thickly sliced

4–6 globe artichoke hearts, cut into quarters

leaves from a bunch of fresh flat leaf parsley, finely chopped

leaves from a bunch of fresh coriander, finely chopped

leaves from a bunch of fresh mint, finely chopped

sea salt and freshly ground black pepper

serves 4–6

Preheat the oven to 200ºC (400ºF) Gas 6.

Tip the couscous into an ovenproof dish. Stir the salt into the water and pour it over the couscous. Leave the couscous to absorb the water for about 10 minutes.

Using your fingers, rub the oil into the couscous grains to break up the lumps and aerate them. Scatter the butter over the surface and cover with a piece of foil. Put in the preheated oven for about 15 minutes, until the couscous is heated through.

Meanwhile, prepare the vegetable broth. Pour the stock into a heavy-based saucepan and bring it to the boil. Add the broad beans, peas, spring onions, courgettes and artichokes and cook for 5–10 minutes, until tender. Season the broth to taste with salt and pepper and stir in the herbs.

Remove the couscous from the oven and tip it onto a serving plate. Using a slotted spoon, lift the vegetables out of the broth and arrange them around, or over, the mound of couscous. Moisten with a little of the broth, then pour the rest into a jug and serve separately to pour over the couscous. Serve immediately.

french bean, pea & new potato salad

450 g new potatoes, washed and halved, if large

a couple of sprigs of fresh mint

4 eggs

4 handfuls of fresh, shelled peas

about 200 g French beans, trimmed

a few handfuls of lettuce leaves

2 tablespoons olive oil

2 teaspoons red wine or cider vinegar

serves 4

Boil the new potatoes in a pan with the sprigs of mint.

Heat a pan of water over medium high heat and bring to the boil. Add the eggs and hard-boil – this should take around 7 minutes. Transfer the pan to the sink and run cold water over the eggs to cool them down. When the eggs are cool, peel off their shells and cut them into quarters.

Boil the peas and French beans. Put in a big salad bowl with the potatoes, eggs and lettuce.

Mix together the olive oil and vinegar, add to the salad and gently mix together.

broad bean, courgette & lemon soup

2 tablespoons extra virgin olive oil

1 unwaxed lemon

1 onion, chopped

3 tablespoons freshly chopped flat leaf parsley, plus extra to serve

500 g courgettes, sliced

300 g broad beans (podded weight)

800 ml vegetable stock

sea salt and freshly ground black pepper

lemon & thyme oil

2 unwaxed lemons

2 fresh thyme or lemon thyme sprigs

250 ml extra virgin olive oil

serves 4

To make the lemon and thyme oil, peel off the lemon zest using a peeler, leaving behind the bitter white pith. Put the zest, thyme and olive oil in a saucepan and heat gently for 10 minutes. Remove from the heat and leave to cool. Season to taste.

For the soup, heat the oil in a large saucepan. Peel the zest from the lemon in one large piece so it's easy to find later and add that to the pan. Add the onion, parsley and courgettes, cover and cook over low heat, stirring occasionally, for 8 minutes or until softening. Remove the lemon zest. Add the beans and stock, season well and return to the heat for a further 20 minutes.

Transfer a quarter of the soup to a blender, liquidize until smooth, then stir back into the soup. Check the seasoning and add lemon juice to taste.

Divide the soup between 4 bowls, drizzle with a little lemon and thyme oil and serve with extra parsley and a grinding of pepper.

Note Any leftover lemon and thyme oil can be stored in a lidded jar in the refrigerator for 2–3 days, and can be used to add flavour to soups and salads.

bean & chickpea salad

450 g green beans

2 tablespoons sake or dry sherry

3 teaspoons sugar

5 teaspoons soy sauce

240 ml vegetable stock

40 g sesame seeds

410-g tin chickpeas, drained

½ teaspoon sesame oil

serves 4

Bring a saucepan of water to the boil, add the beans and cook for 5 minutes until tender but still firm to the bite. Drain and rinse in cold water, then plunge into iced water to set their colour.

Bring the sake to the boil in a small saucepan and then transfer to a bowl and combine with the sugar and soy sauce.

Put the stock in a saucepan with 1 tablespoon of the sake mixture. Bring to the boil. Drain the beans and add to the stock. Return to the boil, then remove from the heat, drain and leave to cool.

Heat a frying pan, add the sesame seeds and toast, keeping them moving, until they are golden. Transfer the seeds to a mortar and pestle or mini food processor and grind them to a rough paste.

In a bowl, combine the ground sesame seeds with the chickpeas, oil and the remaining sake mixture, then toss through the drained beans. Serve immediately.

green beans with a spanish dressing

1 pink banana shallot or 2 large shallots, chopped

2 tablespoons white wine vinegar

1 garlic clove

a pinch of sugar

4 tablespoons extra virgin olive oil

400 g thin green beans

1 hard-boiled egg, finely chopped

1 tablespoon freshly chopped flat leaf parsley

sea salt and freshly ground black pepper

serves 6–8

Put the chopped shallot in a small bowl and add 1 tablespoon of the vinegar and 1 tablespoon water.

Crush the garlic to a paste with the sugar and a pinch of salt. Add pepper and the remaining vinegar and gradually whisk in the oil to make a dressing.

Cook the beans in a saucepan of boiling salted water for about 4 minutes until just cooked but still crisp. Drain and transfer to a serving dish. Pour over the dressing and mix well. Rinse and drain the shallot. Sprinkle the shallot, egg and parsley on top of the beans and serve warm or cold.

florentine green beans

600 g beans, topped and tailed

4 tablespoons extra virgin olive oil

1 medium onion, thinly sliced

1 teaspoon fennel seeds, lightly crushed

1 tablespoon tomato purée

100 ml warm water

sea salt and freshly ground black pepper

serves 4

Bring a saucepan of salted water to the boil and add the beans. Boil for about 6 minutes until tender yet crisp. Meanwhile, heat the oil in a frying pan and cook the onion for about 5 minutes until just beginning to colour and soften. Drain the beans as soon as they are cooked and set aside.

Add the crushed fennel seeds to the onion with plenty of salt and pepper. Mix the tomato purée with the warm water and add to the onion mixture. Bring to the boil and stir in the beans, tossing well to coat with the sauce. Taste and season again. Cover and simmer gently for 5 minutes more, then serve.

french beans with garlic

625 g French beans, trimmed

2 tablespoons olive oil

1 tablespoon unsalted butter

2 garlic cloves, crushed

a handful of fresh flat leaf parsley, chopped

1 teaspoon freshly squeezed lemon juice

sea salt and freshly ground black pepper

serves 4

Bring a large saucepan of water to the boil. Add the beans and cook for 3–4 minutes from the time the water returns to the boil. Drain and refresh under cold running water. Set aside.

Heat the olive oil and butter in a frying pan. Add the garlic, the beans and a little salt, and cook on high for 1 minute, stirring. Remove from the heat and stir in the parsley and lemon juice. Sprinkle with black pepper and serve.

greens & salad vegetables

cauliflower & swiss chard salad

cauliflower gratin 🌿 cauliflower masala

creamy cauliflower & gruyère soup

spaghetti with broccoli, walnuts & ricotta

tenderstem broccoli, shiitake & tofu omelette

braised red cabbage with chestnuts & apples

red cabbage & currant pickle 🌿 cabbage, sprouts

& lettuce sauté 🌿 savoy cabbage with bacon & cream

punjabi cabbage 🌿 creamy coleslaw

baked spinach mornay 🌿 fresh spinach & chickpea curry

sautéed spinach with orange & almonds

spinach & cheese burek

swiss chard, feta cheese & egg pie

swiss chard & brown lentil soup 🌿 chilled lettuce soup

caesar salad 🌿 rocket & fennel salsa verde

The distinctive thick leaves that seem to hug the head of a cauliflower are actually protecting the white 'flower' from the sun. In doing so, they deprive it of what it needs to turn green, and that's essentially the difference between the cauliflower and its close relative broccoli. Cauliflower is often overlooked in favour of other brassicas, such as broccoli, that are quicker to cook. But it has an intense flavour which works so well in this light and spicy Middle Eastern-style salad, and also with creamy cheeses such as in this gratin.

cauliflower & swiss chard salad

65 ml light olive oil

1 small head of cauliflower, separated into large florets

1 teaspoon ground cumin

6 large Swiss chard leaves, chopped into 2-cm wide strips

1 red onion, cut into wedges

2 garlic cloves, chopped

400-g tin chickpeas, rinsed and drained

65 ml tahini (sesame seed paste)

2 tablespoons freshly squeezed lemon juice

¼ teaspoon freshly cracked white pepper

sea salt

serves 4

Put the oil in a frying pan set over high heat, add the cauliflower florets and cook for 8–10 minutes, turning often, until they are a dark, golden brown. Add the cumin and cook, stirring, for 1 minute. Add the Swiss chard, onion and garlic to the pan and cook for a further 2–3 minutes. Add the chickpeas and stir. Season to taste with salt.

Combine the tahini, lemon juice and white pepper in a small bowl and add a little salt to taste. Whisk to combine. Transfer the vegetables to a bowl and drizzle the dressing over the top to serve.

* tip

The secret of delicious cauliflower is to blanch it first; if you parboil it with a bay leaf, the unpleasant cabbage aroma disappears completely.

cauliflower gratin

1 fresh bay leaf

1 large cauliflower, separated into large florets

500 ml double cream

1 egg

2 teaspoons Dijon mustard

160 g Comté cheese, finely grated*

coarse sea salt

a baking dish, about 25 cm diameter, greased with butter

serves 4–6

Bring a large saucepan of water to the boil, add the bay leaf, salt generously, then add the cauliflower florets. Cook for about 10 minutes, until still slightly firm. Drain and set aside.

Put the double cream in a saucepan and bring to the boil. Boil for 10 minutes. Add a spoonful of hot milk to the beaten egg to warm it, then stir the egg, mustard and 1 teaspoon salt into the cream.

Preheat the oven to 200°C (400°F) Gas 6. Divide the cauliflower into smaller florets, then stir them into the cream sauce. Transfer to the prepared baking dish and sprinkle the cheese over the top in an even layer. Bake in the preheated oven for 40–45 minutes, until golden. Serve hot.

Note Like Gruyère, Comté is a mountain cheese – from the Franche-Comté region to be precise – but the similarity stops there. Comté's distinct flavour comes from the milk used in the making, so the flavour varies with the seasons. A springtime diet of tender young shoots delivers milk that is very different from its winter counterpart, nourished mainly on hay: it is darker in colour and fruitier in summer, paler and more nutty in winter. Use Emmental or Cantal if it is unavailable.

Cauliflower makes a substantial meal in itself and these two simple suppers are perfect if you have plenty of produce but not much else in the pantry! In this simple masala, cauliflower florets are stir-fried in a seasoned, spiced oil until just tender. Substitute broccoli florets if desired, to ring the changes. A small, whole head of cauliflower that is creamy-white and soft is best for this soup as the recipe does not involve straining the puréed mixture. Although this dish is somewhere between being a soup and a fondue, it knows exactly what it is – deliciously creamy and cheesy.

cauliflower masala

1 tablespoon sunflower oil

2 teaspoons cumin seeds

1 teaspoon black mustard seeds

500 g cauliflower florets

2 garlic cloves, thinly sliced

2 teaspoons finely chopped fresh ginger

1 green chilli, thinly sliced

1 teaspoon garam masala

150 ml hot water

freshly squeezed juice of ½ lemon

sea salt and freshly ground black pepper

serves 4

Heat the sunflower oil in a large frying pan over medium heat. Add the cumin seeds and mustard seeds. Stir-fry for 30 seconds, then add the cauliflower, garlic, ginger and chilli. Turn the heat to high and stir-fry for 6–8 minutes, or until the cauliflower is lightly browned at the edges.

Stir in the garam masala and hot water and stir well. Cover and cook over high heat for 1–2 minutes.

Season well and drizzle with the lemon juice just before serving.

creamy cauliflower & gruyère soup

2 tablespoons butter

1 onion, roughly chopped

1 celery stick, chopped

1 small cauliflower, about 1 kg, cut into small pieces

1.5 litres vegetable or chicken stock

250 ml double cream

200 g Gruyère cheese, grated, plus extra to serve

sea salt and freshly ground black pepper

freshly chopped parsley and toasted wholemeal bread, to serve

serves 4

Heat the butter in a saucepan over high heat. Add the onion and celery and cook for 5 minutes, until the onion has softened but not browned.

Add the cauliflower pieces and stock and bring to the boil. Allow to boil for 25–30 minutes, until the cauliflower is really soft and breaking up in the stock.

Transfer the mixture to a food processor or blender and process the mixture in batches until smooth. Return the purée to a clean saucepan. Add the cream and cheese and cook over low heat, stirring constantly, until the cheese has all smoothly melted into the soup.

Season to taste with a little sea salt and black pepper. Serve sprinkled with chopped parsley and extra cheese and with buttered wholemeal toast on the side.

Broccoli is a relatively modern vegetable. It was developed in Italy from the now trendy purple sprouting broccoli. There is actually very little to choose between them in taste so it's just a question of whether you prefer the compactness of a head or the leafiness of the sprouting variety. They both get a role in these two perfect midweek-supper dishes. The light texture and creamy flavour of ricotta cheese makes the perfect backdrop to walnuts and broccoli in this deliciously simple and quick pasta dish. The omelette has a distinctly Asian feel with the creamy cubes of tofu replacing the more traditional cheese.

spaghetti with broccoli, walnuts & ricotta

100 g walnut halves

1 head of broccoli, about 400–500 g

3 tablespoons light olive oil

3 garlic cloves, thinly sliced

a handful of fresh flat leaf parsley, chopped

finely grated zest and freshly squeezed juice of 1 unwaxed lemon

200 g fresh ricotta cheese

400 g spaghetti

sea salt and freshly ground black pepper

serves 4

Preheat the oven to 180°C (350°F) Gas 4. Spread the walnuts out on a baking tray and roast in the preheated oven for about 8 minutes, shaking the tray occasionally, until they start to brown.

To prepare the broccoli, trim off the gnarly part, about 2 cm from the stem end, and discard. Thinly slice the stem until you reach the point where it starts to branch into florets. Slice off the individual florets. Heat the oil in a frying pan, add the stems and cook for about 2–3 minutes, turning often, then add the florets and cook for about 5 minutes, until the broccoli has softened. Add the garlic, parsley, lemon zest and walnuts and cook for 5 minutes, stirring often. Reduce the heat to medium and stir through the ricotta and lemon juice. Season well with salt and pepper and leave in the pan to keep warm.

Cook the spaghetti according to the packet instructions. Drain and return it to the warm pan with the sauce. Stir gently to combine and serve immediately.

tenderstem broccoli, shiitake & tofu omelette

1 tablespoon light olive oil

2 shallots, sliced

1 bunch of tenderstem broccoli, chopped into small pieces

200 g shiitake mushrooms

50 g baby spinach leaves

2 teaspoons light soy sauce

300 g firm tofu, cubed

8 eggs, lightly beaten

ground white pepper

oyster sauce, to serve (optional)

serves 4

Put the oil in a large, non-stick frying pan and set over high heat. Add the shallots, broccoli and mushrooms and stir-fry for 3–4 minutes, until the mushrooms are soft and the broccoli turns a bright, emerald green. Add the spinach and cook until just wilted. Add the soy sauce and stir. Arrange the cubes of tofu over the vegetables so that they are evenly spaced. Preheat the grill to high. Pour the beaten eggs into the pan and cook over high heat until the edges have puffed up.

Keep the omelette in the pan, place it under the preheated grill and cook until golden and firm on top. Remove and let cool a little before drizzling with the oyster sauce (if using), then sprinkle with white pepper to serve.

Variation Try replacing the broccoli with young, tender peas and add a sprinkling of fresh coriander.

Red cabbage is a firm winter favourite; it is great for adding colour to dishes, and goes especially well with rich meats. The instant sweet-and-sour pickle is a great quick condiment to have at the ready, especially with sausages, while braised cabbage with apples and chestnuts is a perfect side to a Sunday roast or even a Christmas goose. Serve it with the same wine as used in the cooking.

braised red cabbage
with chestnuts & apples

1 red cabbage

3 tablespoons unsalted butter

1 onion, halved and thinly sliced

75 g bacon lardons

3 cooking apples, peeled, cored and chopped

200 g vacuum-packed whole peeled chestnuts

2 teaspoons coarse sea salt

250 ml dry white wine, preferably Riesling

1 tablespoon sugar

serves 4–6

Cut the cabbage in quarters, then core and slice thinly.

Melt 2 tablespoons of the butter in a frying pan. Add the onion and lardons and cook for about 3 minutes, until soft.

Add the remaining butter, the cabbage, apples and chestnuts and stir well. Season with salt, then add the wine, sugar and 250 ml water.

Bring to the boil, boil for 1 minute, then cover and simmer gently for about 45 minutes, until the cabbage is tender.

red cabbage & currant
pickle

3 tablespoons olive oil

½ small red cabbage, thinly sliced

60 ml red wine

3 tablespoons brown sugar

60 ml balsamic vinegar

35 g currants

35 g pine nuts

makes about 625 ml

Heat the oil in a large frying pan over low to medium heat. Add the cabbage, cover and cook for 5 minutes. Turn up the heat to high, add the wine and let it bubble, then add the sugar, vinegar and currants. Cook, stirring, for 5 minutes.

Heat a frying pan to medium, add the pine nuts and toast, stirring, until golden. Stir the toasted pine nuts into the pickle. Leave to cool and refrigerate until needed. The pickle will keep in the refrigerator for up to 2 weeks.

* tip

Unlike other types of cabbage, red cabbage can be braised slowly and will not spoil from prolonged cooking times. Braised cabbage also freezes very well, which is good news as 1 cabbage will produce several servings. Cook up a batch and store some in the freezer for up to 3 months.

cabbage, sprouts & lettuce sauté

400 g Brussels sprouts

1 tablespoon olive oil

1 tablespoon butter

1 teaspoon caraway seeds

¼ green cabbage, thinly sliced

½ iceberg lettuce, cut into 1-cm slices

freshly squeezed juice of ½ lemon

½ teaspoon sea salt

serves 4–6

Separate as many leaves as you can from the Brussels sprouts and then finely slice any remaining leaves that are too tight to separate. Set aside.

Heat a large sauté pan or wok. Add the oil and butter and heat to medium. Add the caraway seeds and sizzle for about 30 seconds. Add the sprouts and cabbage and stir-fry for about 4 minutes until wilted. Add the lettuce, stir-fry for a further minute, then quickly transfer to a serving dish to stop the cooking. Pour over the lemon juice and sprinkle with the salt. Toss and serve immediately.

savoy cabbage with bacon & cream

1 bay leaf

1 savoy cabbage, about 1.25 kg

2 tablespoons butter

1 tablespoon extra virgin olive oil

100 g thinly sliced pancetta, chopped

a sprig of fresh sage, leaves stripped and thinly sliced

4 tablespoons double cream or crème fraîche

sea salt and freshly ground black pepper

serves 4

Bring a large saucepan of water to the boil with a bay leaf and a large pinch of salt. Quarter the cabbage and blanch in the boiling water for 2–3 minutes. Drain well.

Core the cabbage quarters, then slice crosswise.

Heat the butter and olive oil in a large frying pan. Add the pancetta and sage and cook over high heat, stirring often, for 1 minute. Add the cabbage and a pinch of salt and cook, stirring often, for 2–3 minutes.

Stir in the cream and cook until warmed through, about 1 minute. Season generously with pepper and mix well. Add salt and pepper to taste and serve hot.

punjabi cabbage

3 tablespoons sunflower oil

4 shallots, finely chopped

2 teaspoons finely grated fresh ginger

2 teaspoons crushed garlic

2 green chillies, halved lengthways

2 teaspoons cumin seeds

1 teaspoon ground turmeric

1 teaspoon coriander seeds, crushed

500 g green or white cabbage, shredded

1 tablespoon mild or medium curry powder

1 tablespoon ghee or butter

salt and freshly ground black pepper

serves 4

Heat the sunflower oil in a large, non-stick wok or frying pan over low heat. Add the shallots, ginger, garlic and chillies and stir-fry for 2–3 minutes, or until the shallots have softened.

Add the cumin seeds, turmeric and coriander seeds and stir-fry for 1 minute.

Turn the heat to high and add the cabbage, tossing well to coat in the spice mixture. Add the curry powder and season well. Cover and cook over medium heat for 10 minutes, stirring occasionally. Stir in the ghee and serve.

creamy coleslaw

250 g white cabbage, shredded

175 g carrots, grated

½ white onion, thinly sliced

1 teaspoon salt

2 teaspoons caster sugar

1 tablespoon white wine vinegar

50 g mayonnaise

2 tablespoons double cream

1 tablespoon wholegrain mustard

sea salt and freshly ground black pepper

serves 4

Put the cabbage, carrots and onion in a colander and sprinkle with the salt, sugar and vinegar. Stir well and let drain over a bowl for 30 minutes.

Squeeze out excess liquid from the vegetables and put them in a large bowl. Put the mayonnaise, cream and mustard in a separate bowl and mix well, then stir into the cabbage mixture. Season to taste with salt and pepper and serve. Store in the refrigerator for up to 3 days.

These two deliciously rich dishes prove that spinach is not about dieting or abstinence! The spinach mornay is wonderful for entertaining, ideally served with bread, to soak up the rich sauce, or a simple green salad with a tangy vinaigrette. Also great for guests is this vibrantly-coloured, aromatic curry. Chickpeas are popular in India and work brilliantly here in this dish.

baked spinach mornay

40 g butter

2 tablespoons plain flour

750 ml full-fat milk

200 g Fontina cheese, cubed

1 onion, chopped

1 garlic clove, chopped

1 kg fresh spinach leaves, chopped

¼ teaspoon freshly grated nutmeg

toasted and buttered sourdough bread, to serve (optional)

serves 6

Preheat oven to 180ºC (350ºF) Gas 4. Put 25 g of the butter in a saucepan set over medium heat. When it is melted and sizzling, add the flour and cook for 1 minute, stirring constantly, until a thick paste forms.

Reduce the heat to low and slowly pour the milk into the pan, whisking constantly, until all the milk is incorporated and the mixture is smooth and lump-free. Add the cheese and stir until it has melted into the sauce. Set aside until needed.

Heat the remaining butter in a large frying pan set over high heat, add the onion and garlic and cook for 2–3 minutes, until the onion has softened. Add the spinach, cover with a lid, and cook for 4–5 minutes, stirring often, until the spinach has wilted. Transfer the spinach to a large bowl. Pour in the cheese sauce and stir to combine. Spoon the mixture into a large baking dish.

Sprinkle the nutmeg over the top and bake in the preheated oven for 30 minutes until the top of the mornay is golden and bubbling. Serve on slices of toasted and buttered sourdough bread, if liked.

fresh spinach & chickpea curry

1 white onion, roughly chopped

2 garlic cloves, sliced

1 teaspoon chopped fresh ginger

1 tablespoon light olive oil

2 tablespoons mild curry paste

400-g tin chopped tomatoes

400-g tin chickpeas, well drained and rinsed

500 g fresh spinach, stalks removed and leaves chopped

a handful of fresh coriander leaves, chopped

naan or roti bread, to serve

serves 4

Put the onion, garlic and ginger in a food processor and process until finely chopped. Heat the oil in a frying pan set over high heat. Add the onion mixture and cook for 4–5 minutes, stirring often, until golden. Add the curry paste and stir-fry for just 2 minutes, until aromatic.

Stir in the tomatoes, 250 ml cold water and the chickpeas. Bring to the boil, then reduce the heat to a medium simmer and cook, uncovered, for 10 minutes. Stir in the spinach and cook just until it is wilted.

Stir in the coriander and serve with the Indian bread of your choice.

Garden-fresh spinach forms the basis of these two dishes from diverse cultures. Sautéed with orange and almonds, this Moroccan-inspired side dish is a perfect match for aromatic tagines. While in Eastern Europe, this moreish snack of spinach and cheese enveloped in crisp, golden filo pastry is traditionally enjoyed with a refreshing glass of keffir, a type of drinking yoghurt.

sautéed spinach with orange & almonds

500 g fresh spinach leaves, thoroughly rinsed and drained

2–3 tablespoons olive oil and a knob of butter

1 onion, roughly chopped

2 garlic cloves, finely chopped

freshly squeezed juice and zest of 1 orange

2 tablespoons flaked almonds, toasted

sea salt and freshly ground black pepper

serves 2–4

Put the spinach in a steamer and cook for 8–10 minutes, until soft. Tip the cooked spinach onto a wooden board and chop to a pulp. Set aside.

Heat the oil and butter in a heavy-based saucepan. Stir in the onion and garlic and cook until they begin to colour. Add the spinach and mix until thoroughly combined. Add the orange juice and zest and season to taste with salt and pepper.

Tip the spinach into a serving dish, garnish with the toasted almonds and serve immediately.

spinach & cheese burek

300 g fresh spinach (or 420 g frozen spinach, defrosted and drained)

110 g cottage cheese

100 g Greek yoghurt

1 large egg, beaten

30 ml olive oil, plus extra to brush

30 ml sparkling water

½ teaspoon bicarbonate of soda

1 teaspoon salt

250 g large filo pastry sheets

an 18-cm square brownie tin (4 cm deep), greased

makes 4–6 portions

Preheat the oven to 180°C (350°F) Gas 4.

Blanch the spinach in a saucepan of boiling water for 30 seconds. Drain and squeeze to get rid of excess water. Chop finely, then put in a mixing bowl with the cottage cheese, yoghurt, egg, oil, water, bicarbonate of soda and salt and mix well.

Lay a filo sheet in the base of the brownie tin, leaving the excess pastry hanging over one side of the tin. Brush with oil. Lay another sheet on top so that the overhang is on the opposite side of the tin. Spread a generous tablespoon of spinach mixture over the filo sheet. Lay another 2 sheets over the filling and scrunch up the excess pastry to fit the tin. Brush with oil. Spread another generous tablespoon of spinach mixture over the filo sheet. Lay another 2 sheets over the filling and scrunch up the excess pastry to fit the tin. Brush with oil. Keep going until you've used up the spinach mixture. You should end with a layer of filling.

Finally, fold over the overhanging pastry to cover the top of the burek and brush all over with more oil. If the top isn't entirely covered with pastry, add another sheet and brush with oil.

Bake in the preheated oven for 40 minutes until deep golden and risen. Remove from the oven and leave to cool for a few minutes. It freezes well – defrost and warm up in the oven before serving.

Using fresh, seasonal ingredients simply prepared is the secret of any good recipe. Swiss chard and brown lentils make a perfect combination for hearty soups and casseroles. Or try chard in combination with feta cheese and eggs in this rustic free-form pie, where the pastry is simply rolled out and turned up at the edges rather than formed in a tin.

swiss chard, feta cheese & egg pie

3 tablespoons olive oil

1 red onion, sliced

2 garlic cloves, sliced

500 g Swiss chard, cut into 2-cm pieces

4 eggs

200 g feta cheese, crumbled

sea salt and freshly ground black pepper

pastry

250 g plain flour

150 g unsalted butter, cubed

2 egg yolks

2–3 tablespoons iced water

serves 6

To make the pastry, put the flour and butter in the bowl of a food processor and put the bowl in the freezer for 10 minutes. Pulse the ingredients a few times until just combined. With the motor of the food processor running, add the egg yolks and just enough iced water so that the mixture is on the verge of coming together. Do not overbeat, as this will make the pastry tough. Remove the dough from the bowl and use lightly floured hands to quickly form it into a ball. Wrap in clingfilm and let rest in the fridge for 30 minutes.

Put 2 tablespoons of the oil in a frying pan set over high heat, add the onion and garlic and cook for 2 minutes, until it softens and just flavours the oil. Add the Swiss chard to the pan and cook for about 5 minutes, stirring often, until it wilts and softens. Season well with salt and pepper, leave in the pan and set aside to cool.

Preheat the oven to 220ºC (425ºF) Gas 7. Roll the dough out on a sheet of lightly floured baking paper to form a circle about 35 cm in diameter, trimming away any uneven bits. Roll the edge over to form a 1-cm border, then roll over again. Transfer the pastry circle to a baking tray. Spoon the Swiss chard mixture over the pastry.

Put the eggs in a bowl and prick the yolks with a fork. Pour the eggs over the Swiss chard so that they are evenly distributed, then scatter the feta over the top. Drizzle the remaining oil over the pie and cook in the preheated oven for about 20 minutes, until the pastry is golden and the top of the pie is just starting to turn brown.

Leave to cool for 10 minutes before cutting into slices to serve.

swiss chard & brown lentil soup

1 litre vegetable or chicken stock

280 g dried brown lentils

65 ml olive oil

1 onion, chopped

4 garlic cloves, finely chopped

850 g Swiss chard, trimmed and thinly sliced

65 ml freshly squeezed lemon juice

leaves from a small bunch of fresh coriander, roughly chopped

sea salt and freshly ground black pepper

serves 4

Put the stock and lentils in a large saucepan and bring to the boil. Reduce the heat to medium and cook for 1 hour, uncovered, until the lentils are tender. Reduce the heat to low.

Heat the oil in a large frying pan set over high heat. Add the onion and garlic along with a pinch of salt. Cook for 4–5 minutes, stirring often, until softened.

Stir in the chard and stir-fry for 2–3 minutes, until wilted. Add the chard mixture to the lentils and cook over low heat for 10 minutes.

Stir in the lemon juice and coriander and season to taste with salt and pepper. Serve immediately.

Variation Add diced chicken breast along with the Swiss chard and let it poach gently in the stock.

In the height of summer, cool, clean-tasting soups and fresh crunchy salads are a great way to start a meal. For both recipes use the freshest, just-picked lettuce, and ensure that none has bolted or is oozing a milky substance from the stem, since this may give a bitter taste. Best results are achieved if all the soup ingredients are cold before you start. This means that less chilling time is required and the lettuce will keep its crunch.

chilled lettuce soup

250 g lettuce, cleaned and chopped

250 g yoghurt

1 small garlic clove, crushed with a pinch of coarse salt

1–2-cm piece of fresh ginger, peeled and finely grated

fresh mint leaves

juice of ½ lemon

sea salt and freshly ground black pepper

serves 4

Put all the ingredients into a food processor or blender, adding just enough water to get the blades moving, and blend until the desired consistency is achieved. Blending time varies according to the type of lettuce and the type of machine you are using, but aim to make the soup fairly smooth.

caesar salad

1 cos lettuce

150 ml olive oil

2 large garlic cloves, crushed

2 tablespoons freshly squeezed lemon juice, from about ½ large lemon

½ teaspoon Dijon mustard

2 anchovy fillets in oil, drained

1 large egg yolk

2 slices of stale bread, crusts removed, cubed

2 tablespoons freshly grated Parmesan cheese

sea salt and freshly ground black pepper

serves 4

Pull the leaves off the lettuce, wash and tear into bite-sized pieces. Spin in a salad spinner or dry on kitchen paper. Store in a sealed plastic bag in the refrigerator to keep it crisp.

Put 3 tablespoons olive oil in a blender or food processor and add half the garlic, the lemon juice, mustard, anchovies and egg yolk. Blend until smooth, then transfer to a jug, taste and season with salt and pepper.

Pour the remaining olive oil into a frying pan, add the remaining garlic and heat until it starts to sizzle. Scoop out the garlic, then add the cubed bread. Fry until golden, keeping the pieces on the move while they are cooking. Lift out and drain on kitchen paper.

Stir the dressing, pour over the salad leaves, toss well, then transfer to a bowl. Add the croutons, sprinkle with the Parmesan and serve immediately.

Variation If anchovies don't appeal, liven up the dressing with a dash of Worcestershire sauce. You can use other kinds of salad leaves, such as radicchio, iceberg or Chinese leaves – just remember that they must be crisp to bring out the crunchiness of the salad.

A sharp, pungent and versatile spooning sauce, salsa verde is the perfect foil to rich foods such as ham, pork and salmon. It is also great served with fish, lamb, chicken, potatoes or pasta.

rocket & fennel salsa verde

2 teaspoons fennel seeds

1 garlic clove

1 tablespoon small drained capers

3 anchovy fillets

25 g rocket, chopped

2 tablespoons freshly chopped flat leaf parsley

1 tablespoon freshly squeezed lemon juice

4 tablespoons olive oil

sea salt and freshly ground black pepper

makes about 125 ml

Heat a frying pan over medium heat and add the fennel seeds. Toast them, stirring, for about 1 minute until fragrant. Let cool. Transfer to a mortar and pestle and grind to a rough powder.

Combine the ground fennel seeds, garlic, capers and anchovies in a small bowl and pound until blended. Alternatively, blend them in a mini food processor. Add the rocket, parsley, lemon juice and oil and mix to combine until you have a coarse sauce. Season to taste with salt and pepper. The salsa will keep in the refrigerator for up to 1 week, but it will quickly start to discolour, so is best used when freshly made.

courgettes & squash

pumpkin soup with honey & sage

thai red pumpkin curry 🌿 roasted pumpkin wedges

with lime & spices 🌿 pumpkin & ginger jam

pumpkin & cinnamon filo strudel

butternut squash bread pudding with sweetcorn

roasted squash wedges with pumpkin seed pesto

spaghetti with squash, sage & pecorino

baby squash stuffed with pine nuts & currants

sweet squash, pecan & maple syrup tart

squash & aubergine chutney 🌿 courgette gratin with

herbs & goats' cheese 🌿 courgette & fennel tart

barbecued courgette 🌿 courgettes sautéed with

pancetta & thyme 🌿 minted courgette frittata

honey-roasted courgettes with feta

chocolate & courgette cake

courgette, lemon thyme & feta loaf

Pumpkin and sage are a wonderful combination and make a rich, comforting soup. Instead of fried sage leaves to garnish, you could also try sprinkling over a few toasted pumpkin seeds before serving. This recipe uses vegetable stock, but you could base it on chicken stock, too.

pumpkin soup with honey & sage

75 g unsalted butter

1 small–medium onion, roughly chopped

1 carrot, finely chopped

1 garlic clove, crushed

1 kg pumpkin or butternut squash, deseeded, peeled and cut into cubes

2 heaped tablespoons clear honey

3 sprigs of fresh sage, plus extra crisp-fried leaves (optional), to serve

750 ml vegetable stock

75 ml double cream

freshly squeezed lemon juice, to taste

sea salt and freshly ground black pepper

serves 4–6

Gently melt the butter in a large lidded saucepan or flameproof casserole. Add the onion, carrot and garlic, stir, cover and cook over low heat for about 4–5 minutes. Add the cubed pumpkin, honey and sage, stir, replace the lid and continue to cook very gently for about 10 minutes. Pour in the stock, bring to the boil and cook for a further 10 minutes until the vegetables are soft. Turn off the heat and allow the soup to cool slightly, then remove the sage and strain the soup, retaining the liquid. Put half the cooked vegetables in a food processor with just enough of the reserved cooking liquid to blend into a smooth purée.

Transfer to a clean saucepan and repeat with the remaining vegetables, adding the purée to the first batch. Whizz the remaining liquid in the food processor to pick up the last bits of purée and add that too. Bring the soup slowly to the boil, then stir in the cream without boiling further. Season to taste with lemon juice (about 1 tablespoon), salt (about a teaspoon) and pepper.

Serve with an extra swirl of cream or scatter some crisp-fried sage leaves on top and serve with wholemeal or multigrain bread.

These are two great ways to enjoy pumpkin. Serve spicy wedges on their own or with any roasted or barbecued meat or poultry dish. Save the seeds and roast them lightly with a little oil and coarse salt as a nibble, or in the soup, opposite. You can use butternut squash in this Thai curry instead of the pumpkin if you prefer. To elaborate on the dish for a dinner party, throw in some cooked king prawns 5 minutes before the end of the cooking time.

thai red pumpkin curry

2 tablespoons sunflower oil

1 red onion, thinly sliced

2 garlic cloves, crushed

1 teaspoon finely grated fresh ginger

3 tablespoons Thai red curry paste

800 g pumpkin flesh, cut into bite-sized pieces

400 ml coconut milk

150 ml vegetable stock

6 kaffir lime leaves, plus extra, shredded, to garnish

2 teaspoons grated palm sugar

3 lemongrass stalks, bruised

salt and freshly ground black pepper

Thai sweet basil leaves, to garnish

serves 4

Heat the sunflower oil in a large, non-stick wok or frying pan. Add the onion, garlic and ginger and stir-fry for 3–4 minutes. Stir in the curry paste and pumpkin and stir-fry for 3–4 minutes.

Add the coconut milk, stock, lime leaves, lemongrass and palm sugar. Bring to the boil, then reduce the heat to low and simmer gently for 20–25 minutes, stirring occasionally, or until the pumpkin is tender.

Season well and garnish with the Thai basil leaves and shredded lime leaves just before serving.

roasted pumpkin wedges with lime & spices

1 medium-sized pumpkin, halved lengthways, deseeded, and cut into 6–8 segments

2 teaspoons coriander seeds

1 teaspoon cumin seeds

1 teaspoon fennel seeds

1–2 teaspoons ground cinnamon

2 dried red chillies, chopped

2 garlic cloves

2 tablespoons olive oil

coarse sea salt

finely grated zest of 1 lime

6 wooden or metal skewers, to serve (optional)

serves 6

Preheat the oven to 200°C (400°F) Gas 6.

Using a mortar and pestle, grind all the dried spices with the salt. Add the garlic and a little of the olive oil to form a paste. Rub the mixture over the pumpkin wedges and place them, skin-side down, in a baking dish or roasting tray. Cook them in the preheated oven for 35–40 minutes, or until tender. Sprinkle over the lime zest and serve hot, threaded onto skewers, if using.

pumpkin & ginger jam

1 kg prepared pumpkin, cut into 1–2-cm dice

grated zest and juice of 2 large unwaxed lemons

1 kg granulated sugar

7.5-cm piece of fresh ginger, sliced

500 g cooking apples, peeled, cored and chopped

50 g stem ginger in syrup, drained and cut into shreds

a small piece of muslin

kitchen string

4–5 sterilized jars (see note on page 4)

makes 4–5 small (225 g) jars

In a large non-reactive bowl, layer the pumpkin, lemon zest and sugar. Wrap the fresh ginger and any lemon pips and flesh in a piece of muslin tied with string and bury it in the middle of the pumpkin. Pour over the lemon juice, cover with clingfilm and leave in a cool place for 24 hours, stirring once.

Pour the mixture into a large preserving pan and add the apples. Tie the bag of ginger and lemon mixture to the handle of the pan so that the bag is suspended in the mixture.

Stir over low heat until the sugar completely dissolves, then increase the heat and simmer gently until the pumpkin softens. Increase the heat again and boil vigorously until setting point is reached, about 8–10 minutes*. Stir in the stem ginger. Remove the muslin bag, squeezing it against the side of the pan, then stir in the stem ginger. Let the jam cool for 15 minutes, stir to distribute the ginger, then transfer to hot, dry sterilized jars and seal immediately.

*To test for set, see instructions on page 166.

Here are two perfect recipes for early autumn – a crumbly, heavenly filo strudel made with creamy, sweet pumpkin and a hint of cinnamon, and a fragrant and gloriously amber-coloured preserve. Serve the jam with scones and clotted cream, as a filling for cakes or tarts or with your toast or croissant at breakfast. This recipe makes a softly set jam, which will store well for at least 9 months, but keep in the fridge once opened.

pumpkin & cinnamon filo strudel

200 g pumpkin

½ teaspoon ground cinnamon

50 g golden caster sugar

3 large sheets of thick filo pastry (47 x 32 cm)

20 ml vegetable oil

icing sugar, to dust

a baking tray, greased

makes 6 slices

Preheat the oven to 170ºC (325ºF) Gas 3.

Peel and deseed the pumpkin, then grate the flesh and squeeze out any excess water. Put in a bowl and mix with the cinnamon and caster sugar.

Take one sheet of filo pastry, lay it on the prepared baking tray and lightly brush with oil. Place a second sheet on top and lightly brush with oil. Repeat with the third sheet.

Spoon the pumpkin filling along one longer side of the filo sheets, leaving a 2-cm gap on either side and spreading the filling about 5 cm wide. Fold the longer side of the pastry, nearest the filling, about 2 cm in, then roll the filo pastry up, tucking in the sides as you go. When the strudel is baking, the filling will soften and some juice might seep out, so tucking in the sides ensures that not too much juice is lost.

Brush the top of the strudel with a little more oil and bake in the preheated oven for 25 minutes. The strudel should be pale gold. Remove from the oven and leave to cool for 5 minutes. Dust liberally with icing sugar and serve warm.

One of the simplest and most delicious things you can do with a winter squash is cut it into wedges and roast it. The roasting emphasizes the sweetness and chestnutty denseness of the squash and lends itself to a zesty, full-flavoured pesto such as this one. For something more substantial, try a savoury bread pudding – the sweetness of the squash and sweetcorn go well with the creamy, cheesy bread pudding part. In place of the baguette, you could save up the ends from sliced loaves. And any kind of cheese can be used here, as can a combination of cheeses, so it's a good way to use up odds and ends.

butternut squash bread pudding with sweetcorn

1 tablespoon olive oil

1 large onion, halved and thinly sliced

375 ml milk

225 ml single cream

3 eggs, beaten

a small bunch of fresh chives, snipped

leaves from a small bunch of fresh parsley, finely chopped

1 baguette, cut into ½-cm slices

300 g sweetcorn kernels, freshly shucked, tinned or frozen

about 500 g peeled and sliced butternut squash

100 g mature Cheddar, grated

sea salt and freshly ground black pepper

a 30 x 20 cm baking dish, very well buttered

serves 4–6

Preheat the oven to 190ºC (375ºF) Gas 5.

Heat the oil in a large frying pan. Add the onion and cook over low heat for 3–5 minutes, until soft. Season lightly and set aside.

Combine the milk, cream and eggs in a small bowl and whisk to combine. Season with 1½ teaspoons salt. Add the chives and parsley, mix well and set aside.

Arrange half the baguette slices in the prepared baking dish in a single layer; you may need to tear some to cover all the space. Put half of the onion slices on top, then scatter over half of the sweetcorn. Arrange half of the squash slices evenly on top and sprinkle with half of the cheese. Repeat one more time (bread, onion, sweetcorn, squash, cheese). Stir the milk mixture and pour it evenly all over the pudding.

Cover tightly with foil and bake in the preheated oven for 20 minutes. Remove the foil and continue baking for about 30–40 minutes, until golden. Serve immediately.

roasted squash wedges with pumpkin seed pesto

1 medium-sized winter squash or 2 smaller ones, such as Red Kuri or Butternut, unpeeled

extra virgin olive oil, to drizzle

a few fresh sage leaves

for the pesto

25 g pumpkin seeds

1 garlic clove

a small bunch (about 25 g) of fresh flat leaf parsley

1 small dried red chilli, crumbled, seeds discarded (optional)

25 g semi-dried tomatoes in olive oil, drained

25 g each freshly grated Parmesan cheese and pecorino cheese or 50 g Parmesan

3–4 tablespoons extra virgin olive oil

freshly squeezed lemon juice or 1–2 tablespoons of crème fraîche, to taste

sea salt and freshly ground black pepper

serves 4

Preheat the oven to 200ºC (400ºF) Gas 6.

Cut the squash into wedges, discarding the seeds and pith as you go. Put it on a baking tray, season, drizzle with some olive oil (about 1 tablespoon per wedge) and add a few torn sage leaves. Roast, uncovered, until tender, about 35–40 minutes, turning and basting with the oil once.

Meanwhile, make the pesto. Toast the pumpkin seeds in a dry frying pan over low heat for a few minutes. Do not allow them to burn. In a food processor, process the pumpkin seeds, garlic, parsley, chilli and tomatoes to make a rough paste. Add the cheese and then the oil, enough to make a spoonable pesto. Taste the pesto and add a squeeze of lemon juice to sharpen or crème fraîche to soften the flavour according to taste. Serve immediately with the wedges.

spaghetti with squash, sage & pecorino

65 ml light olive oil

400 g butternut squash, peeled, deseeded and cut into thin wedges

2 garlic cloves, chopped

10–12 small fresh sage leaves

400 g spaghetti

a handful of fresh flat leaf parsley, chopped

50 g pecorino cheese, grated

sea salt and freshly ground black pepper

serves 4

Put the oil in a frying pan and set over high heat. Add the squash and cook for 5–6 minutes, turning often, until golden but not breaking up. Add the garlic and sage to the pan and cook for 2–3 minutes. Remove from the heat and let sit to allow the flavours to develop.

Cook the pasta according to the packet instructions. Drain well and return to the warm pan with the squash mixture. Add the parsley and half of the pecorino and season well with salt and pepper. Serve immediately with the remaining cheese sprinkled over the top.

These two squash dishes are Italian inspired. The baby squash is full of Sicilian flavours, and the unexpected mix of sweet currants with the saltiness of the capers and the cheese is quite wonderful. The lemon and mint lifts the whole thing. Serve it either warm or at room temperature. This tasty pasta is inspired by the classic Italian dish of pumpkin-filled ravioli with sage butter, except this is an inside-out version and therefore much easier to make!

baby squash stuffed with pine nuts & currants

4 small acorn squashes or 4 good-sized courgettes (about 18–20 cm long)

1 tablespoon salted capers

30 g currants

1 medium onion, finely chopped

5–6 tablespoons extra virgin olive oil

2–3 garlic cloves, finely chopped

120 g fresh white breadcrumbs

2 tablespoons freshly chopped flat leaf parsley

2 tablespoons freshly chopped mint leaves

1–2 teaspoons grated lemon zest

50 g Parmesan cheese, freshly grated

50 g pine nuts, lightly toasted

1 egg, beaten (optional)

1 tablespoon freshly squeezed lemon juice

sea salt and freshly ground black pepper

an ovenproof baking dish, oiled

serves 4

If using acorn or other small summer squash, just cut off a thin slice from the base so that they stand upright without wobbling, then cut off a lid and scoop out the seeds to make a cavity. If using courgettes, halve them lengthways and, using a teaspoon, remove the seeds in the centre to leave a 'boat' shape. Season the cut surfaces with salt and leave them upside down to drain. In two separate bowls, cover the capers and currants with warm water and leave them to soak.

When the squashes or courgettes have drained for 45–60 minutes, rinse them, pat dry, then steam for 10–12 minutes until just tender. Drain on kitchen paper. Preheat the oven to 190°C (375°F) Gas 5.

Meanwhile, gently fry the onion in 2 tablespoons of the oil with a pinch of salt until soft and sweet, about 10–15 minutes. Add the garlic and cook for another 3–4 minutes. Drain the capers and currants. Mix the onion and garlic with all the other ingredients except the egg, remaining oil and lemon juice. Season to taste. Stir in the egg for a firmer stuffing, if desired. Put the squash or courgettes in a baking dish and fill the cavities with the stuffing. Mix together the remaining oil and lemon juice and spoon it over the vegetables. Bake in the preheated oven for 30–35 minutes, basting once, until golden and crisp on top. Serve warm with a Greek-style salad.

This tart is one of those rare recipes that tastes just as good, if not better, in reality than on the mind's palate. The squash cuts the rich toffee of the more traditional pecan pie making it softer and more tender. The maple syrup adds a subtle smokiness. You'll need a sweet, orange-fleshed squash or pumpkin here; any of the French or Italian varieties (such as Jaspée de Vendée, Sucrine du Berry or Pleine de Naples) will work, as will Delicata squash. It's best served warm, not hot, with chilled cream or vanilla ice cream.

sweet squash, pecan & maple syrup tart

for the pastry

180 g plain flour

2 tablespoons icing sugar

90 g unsalted butter, chilled

1 egg yolk

1–2 tablespoons freshly squeezed lemon juice

tart filling

25 g unsalted butter

300 g prepared squash or pumpkin, coarsely grated

50 g light muscovado sugar

2 tablespoons bourbon or rum

100 g pecan halves, half chopped

2 eggs

grated zest of 1 unwaxed lemon

150 ml dark maple syrup

½ teaspoon vanilla extract

150 ml double cream

icing sugar, to dust

a deep, 22–23-cm diameter, loose-bottomed metal tart tin

serves 8

To make the pastry, put the flour, icing sugar and butter in a food processor and whizz until the mixture resembles breadcrumbs. Add the egg yolk and sufficient lemon juice, a little at a time, to make a ball of dough. Wrap in foil and chill in the fridge for at least 45 minutes. Roll the dough out on a floured work surface and line the tart tin. Chill for a further 30 minutes. Preheat the oven to 190°C (375°F) Gas 5. Support the sides of the tart with foil and bake in the preheated oven for 12 minutes. Remove the foil, press down any air bubbles in the base and bake for another 10 minutes or until pale brown. Remove from the oven and reduce the heat to 180°C (350°F) Gas 4.

Meanwhile, melt the butter in a frying pan and gently fry the squash for about 5 minutes until tender and lightly browned. Increase the heat a little, add 2 tablespoons of the muscovado sugar and cook until it caramelizes and melts around the squash. Add the bourbon and cook briskly until a sticky syrup forms, then mix in the chopped pecans. Spoon the squash mixture into the tart case and arrange the pecan halves on top. Beat together the eggs, remaining sugar, lemon zest, maple syrup and vanilla extract, then gradually beat in the cream. Pour the mixture into the tart case. Bake in the still-hot oven for about 35–40 minutes, until puffed up and the centre retains a very slight wobble.

This is a golden chutney flecked with the dark purple of the aubergine and the red of the chillies. Substitute white sugar for brown for a deeper colour and flavour.

squash & aubergine chutney

Put the squash and aubergines in a large, stainless steel saucepan with the onions, garlic, chillies, crushed coriander and mustard seeds and the orange zest and juice. Bash the ginger with a rolling pin to bruise it, tie it in a piece of muslin and bury it in the mixture. Pour over the vinegar. Bring to the boil, then simmer very gently, part-covered, for 40–50 minutes until the squash is fully tender. Stir in the warmed sugar and the salt, stir until the sugar dissolves, then bring to the boil and cook briskly, stirring every few minutes, until the mixture is thick and the liquid almost all absorbed, about 30–40 minutes. Stir very frequently towards the end of cooking to prevent the mixture sticking to the base of the pan.

It is ready when a wooden spoon drawn over the base of the pan leaves a clear channel for a few seconds. Adjust the seasoning to taste with salt, cayenne or chilli powder. Leave for 10 minutes, stir well, discard the ginger and then pot into hot, dry sterilized jars. Seal immediately, then invert. Let cool before turning the right way up. Store for at least 4 weeks before using.

Note Either use plastic-covered lids or cellophane discs to cover chutneys, as the vinegar can corrode metal. It will keep for at least 12 months in a cool, dark place. Keep in the fridge once opened.

900 g prepared orange-fleshed squash or pumpkin, cut into 1–2-cm dice

2 large aubergines (about 500 g) cut into 1–2-cm dice

650 g onions, chopped

4 garlic cloves, crushed

2–3 red chillies, deseeded and finely sliced or chopped (leave the seeds in if you want heat)

1 tablespoon each crushed coriander seeds and brown mustard seeds

finely shredded zest and juice of 1 unwaxed orange

50 g fresh ginger

400 ml cider vinegar or white wine vinegar

400 g granulated sugar, warmed

2 teaspoons salt, plus extra to taste

cayenne or chilli powder, to taste

a small piece of muslin
kitchen string
4–5 sealable, sterilized jars (see note on page 4)

makes 4–5 medium (350 g) jars

courgette gratin with herbs & goats' cheese

250 ml double cream

leaves from a small bunch of fresh flat leaf parsley, finely chopped

a small bunch of fresh chives, snipped

a pinch of freshly grated nutmeg

75 g Gruyère, grated

1.5 kg courgettes, very thinly sliced

150 g soft goats' cheese

sea salt and freshly ground black pepper

a 24-cm round, deep-sided baking dish, well buttered

serves 4

A classic of French home cooking, this gratin includes a topping of tangy goats' cheese. If you grow your own herbs, add whatever is available: savory, majoram, oregano or any other soft-leaved herb, the more the merrier. This is perfect simply served with a mixed salad of lettuce and ripe tomatoes and a big basket of fresh crusty bread.

Preheat the oven to 190ºC (375ºF) Gas 5.

Put the cream, parsley, chives, nutmeg, salt and pepper in a small bowl and whisk together. Add half the Gruyère.

Arrange half the courgette slices in the prepared baking dish, sprinkle with the remaining Gruyère and season with a little salt. Top with the remaining courgette slices, season again and pour over the cream mixture. Crumble the goats' cheese over the top.

Bake in the preheated oven for 35–45 minutes, until browned. Serve immediately with a mixed salad and plenty of crusty bread.

Note If preferred, you can make the gratin in 4 individual dishes, simply reduce the cooking time by about 5–10 minutes.

* tip

The courgette has many wonderful uses – both cooked and raw (try them grated into salads), savoury and sweet (they are a wonderful way to keep a sponge moist – see page 127). But what many people don't realise is that courgette blossoms can be eaten along with the vegetable. Before they are harvested, the female flowers develop into little courgettes; use these when the flowers are large and eat both parts. Try stuffing the flowers with soft cheese, coating them in a light batter and frying – delicious.

Fresh and summery, serve this delicious courgette and fennel tart with a rocket salad, fish and white wine for a perfect summer picnic.

courgette & fennel tart

1 Pizza Dough recipe
(see page 56)

350 g courgettes, sliced
1 cm thick

200 g fennel, trimmed and
sliced 1 cm thick

1 small red onion, sliced
5 mm thick

40 ml olive oil

1 teaspoon salt

½ teaspoon crushed black
pepper

1 tablespoon freshly chopped
parsley

100 g mature Cheddar, grated

150 g Greek yoghurt

a 10 x 33-cm tart tin, greased

makes about 6 portions

Preheat the oven to 200ºC (400ºF) Gas 6.

Put the courgettes, fennel, onion, oil, salt and pepper in a roasting tin and toss until evenly combined. Cover the tin with aluminium foil. Roast in the preheated oven for 30 minutes. Remove from the oven, leave covered, and leave to cool for 10–15 minutes.

Reduce the oven temperature to 170ºC (325ºF) Gas 3.

Drain any excess juice from the vegetables, then mix in the parsley and 60 g of the cheese.

Line the tart tin with the Pizza Dough but do not trim the edges yet.

Mix the yoghurt and remaining cheese in a bowl, then pour into the tart shell. Scatter the roasted vegetables over the top, spreading them evenly. Bake in the hot oven for 25–30 minutes. Remove from the oven and leave to cool.

barbecued courgette

8 courgettes, cut lengthways into 1-cm slices

olive oil

balsamic vinegar

salt and freshly ground black pepper

serves 8

Cook the courgette slices over medium heat on a preheated barbecue for 3–4 minutes on each side, until lightly charred. Remove to a plate and sprinkle with oil, vinegar, salt and pepper. Serve hot, warm or cold.

courgettes sautéed with pancetta & thyme

500 g courgettes

3 tablespoons olive oil

75 g pancetta cubes or lardons

1 tablespoon freshly chopped thyme

sea salt (optional) and freshly ground black pepper

freshly squeezed juice of ½ lemon

serves 4

Trim the courgettes and cut into cubes. Heat the oil in a frying pan, add the pancetta and fry until golden. Add the courgettes and fry over brisk heat for 3–4 minutes, tossing them around the pan from time to time until the cut sides start to turn golden.

When golden, add the thyme and plenty of black pepper (you probably won't need any salt). Season with a squeeze of lemon juice and serve immediately.

minted courgette frittata

6 large eggs

2 tablespoons freshly chopped mint

250 g baby new potatoes, thickly sliced

2 tablespoons olive oil

1 large onion, chopped

4 courgettes, sliced

sea salt and freshly ground black pepper

serves 3–4

Break the eggs into a bowl and whisk briefly with a fork. Season well with salt and pepper. Mix in the chopped mint.

Cook the potatoes in a saucepan of boiling, salted water until just tender. Drain thoroughly.

Meanwhile, heat the oil in a frying pan, add the onion and cook gently for about 10 minutes, until soft and pale golden. Add the courgettes and stir over low heat for 3–4 minutes until just softened. Add the potatoes and mix gently.

Pour the eggs over the vegetables and cook over low heat until the frittata is lightly browned underneath and has almost set on top. Slide under a preheated grill for 30–60 seconds, to set the top.

honey-roasted courgettes with feta

500 g courgettes, deseeded if large, cut into chunky batons

2 garlic cloves, sliced

3 tablespoons extra virgin olive oil

200 g feta cheese, coarsely crumbled

2 tablespoons runny honey

freshly ground black pepper

a large ovenproof dish

serves 4

Preheat the oven to 220°C (425°F) Gas 7.

Put the courgettes into a large ovenproof dish in a single layer. Add the garlic and sprinkle with 2 tablespoons of olive oil. Using your hands, toss the courgettes until they are evenly coated with the garlic and oil.

Spread out the courgettes evenly in the dish. Scatter the feta over them and trickle with the remaining olive oil, honey and pepper. The saltiness of the feta means that no extra salt is needed. Roast in the preheated oven until deep golden. Transfer to a serving dish and serve immediately.

If you have an excess of courgettes, they make an excellent baking ingredient – and there is a lovely retro charm, redolent of 1950s cookbooks, about making sweet cakes with a vegetable that's usually served savoury. The courgette in both these recipes performs the same function as grated carrot does in the more familiar carrot cake, keeping the sponge wonderfully moist.

chocolate & courgette cake

250 g butter, softened

250 g light brown soft sugar

2 teaspoons vanilla extract

3 eggs

125 ml milk

350 g self-raising flour

1 teaspoon baking powder

4 tablespoons cocoa powder

450 g courgettes, peeled and grated

a cake tin, 30 x 20 cm, buttered and lined

makes about 20 squares

Preheat the oven to 180°C (350°F) Gas 4.

Put the softened butter, sugar and vanilla extract into a bowl and beat with a wooden spoon or electric whisk until creamy.

Crack the eggs into a bowl and beat lightly with a fork. Add the eggs gradually to the bowl with the cake batter. Add the milk and whisk together.

Put a sieve over your mixing bowl and carefully pour in the flour, baking powder and cocoa powder. Shake the sieve gently so that the ingredients snow down into the bowl. Take a metal spoon and 'fold' into the batter. Stir in the grated courgettes and mix well.

Spoon the cake batter into your tin and bake in the preheated oven for 35–45 minutes. Test the centre of the cake with a skewer – when it comes out clean the cake is ready. Remove the cake from the tin and leave to cool, then cut into squares.

courgette, lemon thyme & feta loaf

325 g plain flour

2 tablespoons baking powder

1 teaspoon salt

200 ml whole milk

150 ml extra virgin olive oil

2 eggs, beaten

1 large courgette, topped, tailed and coarsely grated

125 g feta, crumbled

2 fresh lemon thyme sprigs, leaves only

freshly ground black pepper

a 900-g loaf tin, lined with non-stick baking paper

makes a 900-g loaf

Preheat the oven to 180°C (350°F) Gas 4.

Sift the flour, baking powder and salt into a large bowl and season with freshly ground black pepper.

In a measuring jug, combine the milk and oil and beat in the eggs. Stir into the dry ingredients along with the courgette, two-thirds of the feta and half the thyme leaves. Stir until there are no more floury pockets but don't overbeat it or you'll make the mixture tough. Spoon into the prepared loaf tin. Scatter over the remaining feta and remaining thyme. Bake in the preheated oven for 1–1¼ hours, or until a skewer inserted in the centre comes out clean.

Remove from the oven and leave to cool for 10 minutes in the tin, then turn out onto a wire rack to cool completely.

mushrooms

roasted mushrooms with spiced squash stuffing

mushroom soup with madeira & hazelnuts

mushroom & thyme ragu with

hand-torn pasta ❧ mushroom tart

baked mushrooms with manchego béchamel

sautéed mushrooms & lentils with bacon

garlic mushrooms & goats' cheese on toast

These two dishes are full of warm, comforting flavours. Serve the roasted mushrooms with rice pilaf and maybe a spinach salad. Use a squash with a dryish, chestnutty flesh such as Kabocha or Crown Prince. Mushrooms and their earthiness blend really well with the sweet tang of Madeira wine, with the hazelnuts adding a lovely thickness to the soup.

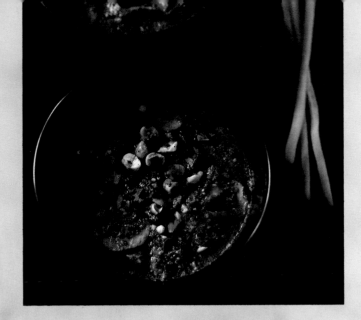

roasted mushrooms with spiced squash stuffing

1 small squash (about 900 g), peeled, deseeded and diced

5–6 tablespoons olive oil

a small bunch of fresh thyme

¼ teaspoon dried chilli flakes

1 garlic clove, chopped

1 x 400-g tin chickpeas, drained

½–1 teaspoon ground toasted cumin seeds

freshly squeezed lemon juice, to taste

1–2 tablespoons chopped flat leaf parsley

1–2 tablespoons crème fraîche (optional)

8 large, flat portobello mushrooms, stalks removed

4 tablespoons toasted pumpkin seeds

sea salt and freshly ground black pepper

for the sauce

1 garlic clove

a pinch of coarse sea salt

3–4 tablespoons tahini

freshly squeezed lemon juice, to taste

4–5 tablespoons natural yoghurt

1 tablespoon freshly chopped mint

serves 4

Preheat the oven to 220°C (425°F) Gas 7. Toss the squash with 3 tablespoons of the oil, 1 teaspoon chopped thyme, the chilli flakes and garlic. Season and put on a baking tray. Cover with foil and cook in the preheated oven for about 30 minutes until tender, then uncover and cook for a further 10 minutes. Leave to cool and put in a food processor with the chickpeas. Whizz to make a rough purée. Season to taste with salt, pepper, cumin and lemon juice, then stir in the parsley. If the purée is very dry, add the crème fraîche or a little water.

Meanwhile, put the mushrooms, gill-side uppermost, on an oiled baking tray. Season and sprinkle with a few thyme leaves. Drizzle with the remaining oil and a good squeeze of lemon juice. Roast, uncovered, in the preheated oven for 15 minutes until just cooked. Remove from the oven and reduce the heat to 190°C (375°F) Gas 5.

Distribute the stuffing evenly between the mushrooms. Scatter with the pumpkin seeds and a few thyme sprigs. Spoon over a little of the mushroom cooking juices, then return them to the oven for 10 minutes to heat through. To make the sauce, mash the garlic with the salt in a bowl, then gradually work in 3 tablespoons tahini, followed by 1 tablespoon lemon juice. When smooth, gradually work in the yoghurt, then taste and add more lemon juice and/or tahini as necessary. Stir in the mint and serve with the mushrooms.

mushroom soup with madeira & hazelnuts

50 g butter

1 large onion, chopped

3 garlic cloves, crushed

25 g blanched hazelnuts

3 tablespoons freshly chopped parsley

350 g chestnut or field mushrooms, sliced

25 g dried porcini mushrooms

1 litre hot vegetable or chicken stock

100 ml Madeira

serves 4–6

Melt the butter in a large saucepan and add the onion and garlic. Cover and cook over low heat for 10 minutes, or until soft. Stir occasionally so that they don't colour. Meanwhile, toast the hazelnuts in a dry frying pan and roughly chop, then set aside.

Add half the parsley and all the mushrooms to the saucepan and turn the heat up to medium. Cover and cook, stirring, for 15 minutes until they are softened.

Put the dried mushrooms in a heatproof bowl with 100 ml of the hot stock and set aside to soak for about 15 minutes to rehydrate.

Add the Madeira to the pan and cook until it evaporates. Add the remaining stock and the dried mushrooms with their soaking liquid, cover and cook for 10 minutes.

Transfer half the soup to a blender, along with half the hazelnuts and liquidize until smooth, then stir back into the pan and heat through. Divide the soup between 4–6 bowls and scatter the remaining parsley and toasted hazelnuts over the top.

Many exotic mushroom varieties are available year-round. These recipes use a mixture, giving the dishes a roundness of flavour. In the pasta, the meaty field mushrooms go hand in hand with the other comforting, rich flavours like fresh thyme, red wine and cinnamon. If you like to pick your own mushrooms, feel free to experiment with your selection, but you can just as easily use any seasonal variety you might find at your local farmers' market.

mushroom tart

1 Pizza Dough recipe
(see page 56)

15 g dried porcini mushrooms

1 large red onion, diced

2 tablespoons olive oil,
plus extra to drizzle

2 tablespoons water

1 teaspoon salt

½ teaspoon crushed black
pepper

1 teaspoon freshly chopped
thyme, plus extra whole sprigs
to decorate

2 garlic cloves, chopped

150 g button mushrooms
(halved if big)

200 g field mushrooms, sliced
about 8 mm thick

180 ml single cream

1 large egg, beaten

*a 20 x 30-cm fluted tart tin,
greased*

serves 6

Put the porcini mushrooms in a bowl of warm water and leave to soak for 20 minutes. Drain, chop and set aside.

Preheat the oven to 200ºC (400ºF) Gas 6.

Put the onion, oil and water in a frying pan and sauté over low heat for about 10 minutes, or until soft and the water has evaporated. Remove from the heat and stir in the salt, pepper, thyme, garlic and porcini mushrooms. Mix well and set aside.

Put the button and field mushrooms in a roasting tray, drizzle with oil and cover the tray with aluminium foil. Roast in the preheated oven for 10 minutes. Remove from the oven and leave to cool for 10 minutes. Drain any excess juice from the mushrooms, then stir them into the onion mixture.

Reduce the oven temperature to 170ºC (325ºF) Gas 3.

Line the tart tin with the Pizza Dough but do not trim the edges yet.

Mix together the cream and egg in a bowl, then pour half into the tart shell. Spread the mixed vegetables over the tart, then pour in the remaining cream mixture. Now trim the excess pizza dough neatly around the edges.

Bake in the preheated oven for 25–30 minutes. Remove from the oven and leave to cool, then decorate with a few sprigs of thyme. Serve warm or cold.

mushroom & thyme ragu
with hand-torn pasta

2 tablespoons light olive oil

2 tablespoons butter

1 onion, chopped

2 garlic cloves, chopped

3 large field mushrooms, caps
removed and cut into 2-cm
pieces

200 g button mushrooms

100 g fresh shiitake
mushrooms, quartered

3 fresh thyme sprigs

250 ml red wine

1 cinnamon stick

250 ml vegetable or beef stock

400 g fresh lasagne sheets,
cut or torn into thick strips

sea salt and freshly ground
black pepper

freshly grated Parmesan
cheese, to serve

serves 4

Heat the oil and butter in a heavy-based saucepan over medium heat. Add the onion and garlic and cook for 4–5 minutes, until the onions have softened. Increase the heat to high, add the mushrooms and thyme and cook for a further 8–10 minutes, stirring often, until the mushrooms darken and soften.

Add the red wine and cinnamon to the pan and boil for 5 minutes. Pour in the stock and season well with sea salt and black pepper. Reduce the heat and gently simmer the mixture for 35–40 minutes.

Cook the pasta in a saucepan of boiling water for 2–3 minutes, until it rises to the surface. Drain well and place in serving bowls. Spoon the mushroom sauce on top and sprinkle with Parmesan to serve.

Tapas is casual, shared food at its very best and mushrooms are very well suited to the small plates style of cooking. They really are nature's cups just waiting to be filled. Look for mushrooms that will be two to three small mouthfuls when cooked – wild field mushrooms or the large portobello mushrooms are both ideal. These are very rich, so a crisp fennel salad is the perfect accompaniment.

baked mushrooms with manchego béchamel

Put the butter in a small saucepan and cook over high heat until it is melted and sizzling. Before the butter burns, add the flour and stir quickly to form a thick paste. Remove from the heat and add a little of the milk, stirring constantly until thick and smooth. Return the pan to medium heat and add the remaining milk, whisking constantly until all the milk is incorporated and the mixture is smooth and thick. Remove from the heat and leave cool.

Preheat the oven to 220°C (425°F) Gas 7. Remove the stalks from the mushrooms and sit the mushrooms in a small baking dish, gill-side up. Spoon the cheese sauce into the caps and sprinkle the paprika over the top. Cook in the preheated oven for 20 minutes, until the mushrooms are soft and the sauce is golden and bubbling.

While the mushrooms are cooking, slice the fennel bulb as finely as possible, chop the fronds and put in a bowl with the parsley, oil and lemon juice. Toss to combine, season to taste and serve with the warm mushrooms.

2 teaspoons butter

2 teaspoons plain flour

125 ml full-fat milk

50 g Manchego cheese, finely grated

12 wide, flat field mushrooms

¼ teaspoon smoked paprika (pimentón)

fennel salad

1 small fennel bulb

a handful of fresh flat leaf parsley leaves

2 teaspoons olive oil

2 teaspoons freshly squeezed lemon juice

sea salt and freshly ground black pepper

serves 4–6

 tip

Although mushroom types are detailed for guidance, the different mushroom varieties can often be used interchangeably, so you can work around what you have available. If you need to slice a lot of mushrooms, try using an egg slicer to make quick work of the job.

The rich, earthy taste of mushrooms makes them perfect for these two rustic dishes. Mushrooms and lentils go fabulously with pork in this hearty hotpot. Small brown lentils stay firm during cooking, but the big green ones called castellanas have a good flavour too. For a quick brunch, garlicky mushrooms are great partnered with soft, creamy goats' cheese. The kind of cheese you are looking for is a soft fresh cheese, not aged, so it will not have a rind. You could also use ricotta if you like. Seek out a good, sturdy rustic bread such as sourdough for this dish to prevent the underneath going soggy.

sautéed mushrooms
& lentils with bacon

250 g small lentils, rinsed

3 tablespoons extra virgin olive oil

1 onion, finely chopped

1 garlic clove, crushed

25 g butter

100 g small chestnut mushrooms

100 g oyster mushrooms, cut in half if large

3 tablespoons freshly chopped flat leaf parsley

1 teaspoon freshly squeezed lemon juice

fine sea salt and freshly ground black pepper

6–12 slices streaky bacon

leaves from a small bunch of fresh flat leaf parsley, half chopped, the rest left whole, to serve

serves 6

Put the lentils in a saucepan, cover with 1 litre cold water and bring to the boil. Lower the heat and simmer for about 35 minutes or until tender (the time will depend on the age of the lentils). Drain.

Heat 2 tablespoons of the oil in a frying pan, add the onion and garlic and fry for about 10 minutes until soft and pale golden. Add the butter, the remaining oil and the mushrooms. Stir-fry until the mushrooms are just cooked. Add the lentils, chopped parsley, lemon juice, salt and pepper and continue to stir until heated all the way through.

Meanwhile, grill the bacon until crisp. Serve the lentils topped with the parsley and 1–2 slices of bacon per serving.

garlic mushrooms &
goats' cheese on toast

8 field mushrooms

3 garlic cloves, crushed

3 tablespoons olive oil

25 g pine nuts

2 tablespoons balsamic vinegar

4 slices of sourdough bread

150 g fresh goats' cheese

fresh tarragon, to serve

sea salt and freshly ground black pepper

serves 4

Preheat the oven to 200°C (400°F) Gas 6.

Put the mushrooms, garlic and oil in a roasting tray. Toss well and season. Roast in the preheated oven for 15 minutes, until tender. Stir in the pine nuts and balsamic vinegar halfway through roasting.

Just before the mushrooms are ready, toast the slices of sourdough bread and spread with the goats' cheese. Place the mushrooms on top, stalk side up, scatter with the tarragon and serve immediately. Add more seasoning, if necessary.

tree fruits

praline apple strudel ❧ apple & blueberry tarts
apple & carrot bread with walnuts ❧ apple, pear &
ginger chutney ❧ **apple, red onion & dried cherry
chutney** ❧ apple butter ❧ **apple lemonade**
toffee apples ❧ **roast apples & parsnips**
poached pear tiramisù ❧ **individual pear, maple &
pecan cobblers** ❧ frosted pear, courgette &
carrot cake ❧ **pickled pears with tamarind & ginger**
roasted pear relish ❧ **warm pear, gorgonzola & pecan
tartlets with maple drizzle** ❧ pan plum crumble
plum fudge puddings ❧ greengage jam
plum & apple tart ❧ free-form caramelized peach tart
roasted mascarpone peaches ❧ peach halves in brandy
with star anise ❧ **upside-down peach cake**
nectarine, blueberry & lavender tray bake
nectarine & pistachio summer crumble
buttered apricot betty ❧ **apricot & almond slump**
white chocolate & apricot roulade ❧ **cherry, peach &
vanilla shortcake** ❧ cherry & ricotta strudel
cherry & almond clafoutis ❧ italian fig conserve
spiced muscat figs

The end of the summer needn't mean the end of gloriously fresh, vibrant desserts. The chances are that your apple trees will be laden with fruit, so here are apples two ways – in individual tarts, using sweet eating apples and juicy blueberries, combined with vanilla; and in a rustic strudel, which is lifted well above the ordinary with the addition of it's secret ingredient – praline powder.

praline apple strudel

450 g tart eating apples, such as Cox's or Braeburn, peeled, cored and chopped

75 g dried fruit, such as sultanas, cranberries or sour cherries

100 g light brown sugar

1 teaspoon ground cinnamon

1 tablespoon unsalted butter

6 sheets filo pastry (thawed if frozen)

50 g unsalted butter, melted

icing sugar, to dust

whipped cream or crème fraîche, to serve

for the praline

75 g shelled pecans

40 g caster sugar

a baking tray, lined with baking paper

serves 6–8

To make the praline, combine the pecans and sugar in a non-stick heavy-based frying pan and cook over medium/high heat, stirring constantly, until the sugar hardens and coats the nuts. Transfer to a plate to cool, then process in a coffee grinder or small food processor until ground to a coarse powder. Set aside.

In a large saucepan, combine the apples, dried fruit, brown sugar, cinnamon and 1 tablespoon butter. Cook over medium heat until the apples are soft and the juices have evaporated, about 15 minutes. Remove from the heat and leave to cool.

Preheat the oven to 190ºC (375ºF) Gas 5.

Put 2 sheets of filo on the prepared baking tray and brush with some melted butter. Sprinkle with a little praline. Top with 2 more sheets of filo and repeat. Top with 2 more sheets of filo. Spread the apple mixture in an even layer over the top sheet of filo. Sprinkle with more praline mixture, then carefully roll up from a long end, like a Swiss roll. Use the paper to help you roll, if necessary. The seam side needs to be on the bottom. Brush with a little more melted butter, sprinkle with any remaining praline and bake in the preheated oven until crisp and golden, about 25–35 minutes.

Remove from the oven and let cool slightly. Dust with a little icing sugar, slice and serve warm with whipped cream or crème fraîche.

apple & blueberry tarts

375 g ready-rolled puff pastry, defrosted if frozen, cut into 4 squares each about 12 cm square

2 tablespoons sugar

1 vanilla pod, cut in half lengthways

3 sweet dessert apples, cored and cut into 10–12 thin wedges

1 punnet blueberries (about 150 g)

cream, to serve

a baking tray, lined with baking paper

serves 4

Preheat the oven to 220ºC (425ºF) Gas 7.

Place the puff pastry squares on a the prepared baking sheet.

Put the sugar and 2 tablespoons water in a saucepan and bring to the boil, stirring until the sugar dissolves. Scrape the seeds from the vanilla directly into the sugar syrup, stirring to combine.

Add the apple slices to the pan, reduce the heat to medium and cook for 4–5 minutes, turning the apples so they cook evenly. Add the blueberries and gently stir to coat in the sweet syrup. Arrange the apples and blueberries on top of each pastry square. Bake in the preheated oven for 18–20 minutes, until the pastry is puffed and golden.

Serve warm with the cream spooned over the top.

This delicious, rustic autumnal bread is very simple to make. One large loaf goes a long way and keeps well, so it is ideal if you just want something freshly baked around the house for a few days. It is very nice plain, or spread with butter or cream cheese if you are feeling indulgent.

apple & carrot bread with walnuts

Preheat the oven to 180°C (350°F) Gas 4.

In a mixing bowl, combine the flour, sugar, baking powder, salt, cinnamon, nutmeg, ginger and allspice. Set aside.

In a separate bowl, mix together the apple juice, melted butter and eggs. Gently fold this mixture into the flour mixture to combine. Use your hands to squeeze every last drop of moisture from the grated apple and carrots then add to the mixture, along with the walnuts and stir just to combine.

Transfer the mixture to the prepared loaf tin and level the top. Bake in the preheated oven until a skewer inserted in the centre of the cake comes out clean, about 1–1¼ hours.

Leave the cake to cool in the tin for a few minutes then turn out onto a wire rack to cool. Slice as you would bread to serve. The cake will keep in an airtight container for 4–5 days.

250 g plain flour

150 g light muscovado sugar

1 tablespoon baking powder

a pinch of fine sea salt

1 teaspoon ground cinnamon

½ teaspoon ground nutmeg

¼ teaspoon each ground ginger and allspice

100 ml apple juice

75 g unsalted butter, melted

2 large eggs, beaten

1 large tart cooking apple, such as Bramley, peeled, cored and grated

100 g grated carrots

65 g walnuts, coarsely chopped

a 23 x 13 x 8-cm loaf tin (900 g capacity), buttered

serves 6–8

Homemade chutneys are very useful to keep on hand. A great way to use fresh produce, they are ideal served with cheese and biscuits or as part of a ploughman's lunch, and they are perfect with roast meats – both hot and cold. They also make a tasty sandwich ingredient. The apple, pear and ginger chutney is especially suited to pork, while the apple, red onion and dried cherry chutney goes very well with chicken, turkey and even duck.

apple, pear & ginger chutney

3 eating apples, such as Golden Delicious, peeled, cored and diced

2 large ripe pears, peeled, cored and diced

1 large white onion, finely chopped

375 ml cider vinegar

350 g light brown sugar

100 g sultanas or raisins

140-g piece of fresh ginger, peeled and finely chopped

½ teaspoon sea salt

½ teaspoon dried red chilli flakes

makes 1–1.5 litres

In a large non-reactive saucepan, combine the apples, pears, onion, vinegar, sugar, sultanas, ginger, salt and chilli flakes. Cook over medium heat, stirring occasionally, until thick, about 30–40 minutes.

Transfer the chutney to a spotlessly clean and dry, sealable airtight container. It will keep in the fridge for up to 2 weeks.

apple, red onion & dried cherry chutney

3 eating apples, such as Golden Delicious, peeled, cored and diced

1 large or 2 medium red onions, halved and sliced

175 g dried sour cherries

500 ml cider vinegar

3 tablespoons light brown sugar

¼ teaspoon ground cloves

¼ teaspoon sea salt

freshly ground black pepper

makes 500–750 ml

In a large non-reactive saucepan, combine the apples, onion, dried cherries, vinegar, sugar, cloves, salt and a few grinds of black pepper. Cook over medium heat, stirring occasionally, until thick, about 30–40 minutes.

Transfer the chutney to a spotlessly clean and dry, sealable airtight container. It will keep in the fridge for up to 2 weeks.

apple butter

1.5 kg mixed apples, such as Braeburn, Cox's and Bramley, peeled, cored and chopped

350 g runny honey

200 g sugar

2 tablespoons freshly squeezed lemon juice

1 teaspoon ground cinnamon

½ teaspoon ground cloves

250 ml apple juice

makes about 2 kg

Combine all the ingredients in a large non-reactive saucepan. Bring to the boil, stirring occasionally. Lower the heat and simmer, stirring occasionally, and using a wooden spoon, crush the apples, until thick, about 20–25 minutes. Remove from the heat.

Transfer the jam to a spotlessly clean and dry, sealable airtight container. It will keep in the fridge for 7–10 days. Alternatively, spoon into hot, dry sterilized jars while hot (see note on page 4). Leave to cool, then seal. The jam will keep for 3–4 weeks if correctly sealed. Use as you would any fruit preserve.

apple lemonade

2–3 cooking apples, unpeeled, chopped into small pieces

sugar, to taste

juice of 1 lemon

ice, to serve

sparkling mineral water, to serve

serves 4

Put the apples into a saucepan, cover with cold water, bring to the boil and simmer until soft. Strain, pressing the pulp through the strainer with a spoon. Add sugar to taste, stir until dissolved, then leave to cool.

To serve, fill a jug with ice, half-fill the glass with the apple juice, add the lemon juice and top with mineral water.

toffee apples

8 small apples, such as Cox's

300 g caster sugar

2 tablespoons golden syrup

freshly squeezed juice of ½ lemon

finely chopped mixed nuts

and edible sprinkles, for dipping (optional)

8 wooden skewers or lolly sticks

a large sheet of non-stick baking paper

makes 8

Wash and thoroughly dry each apple. Carefully push a wooden skewer or lolly stick into the stalk end of each apple.

Put the sugar, golden syrup and 150 ml water in a heavy-based saucepan set over low heat. Leave until the sugar has completely dissolved then turn up the heat and simmer until the toffee turns an amber colour.

Remove the pan from the heat. Add the lemon juice – taking care as the hot toffee may splutter. Working quickly, dip each apple into the toffee and swirl it around until evenly coated.

Leave to cool for 30 seconds, then dip the bottoms of the apples in mixed nuts or sprinkles, if using. Sit the apples on the baking paper to harden. Serve on the same day.

roast apples & parsnips

2 tablespoons olive oil

½ teaspoon dried sage

½ teaspoon salt

1 eating apple, cut into wedges

2 parsnips, about 350 g, peeled and cut into wedges

1 tablespoon freshly chopped flat leaf parsley

serves 4

Preheat the oven to 220°C (425°F) Gas 7.

Put the oil, sage and salt in a plastic bag, then add the apple and parsnips. Roll them around until well coated with oil. Empty the bag onto a baking tray and roast in the preheated oven for 30 minutes, turning the vegetables every 10 minutes. Sprinkle with parsley, mix well and serve.

Tiramisù (which literally translates from the Italian as pick-me-up) must be one of the best-loved desserts in the world. It has all the essential elements of a perfect pudding – alcohol, creamy custard and cocoa. Pears work particularly well with anything sweet, creamy and cheesey so mascarpone makes an ideal partner. Do choose your pears carefully. Soft and sweet varieties, such as Packham, do not poach well and will end up as an overly sweet mush. Bosc are good, but any firm brown variety will work.

poached pear tiramisù

6–8 sponge fingers (savoiardi)

250 ml Marsala or brandy

115 g caster sugar

2 firm brown pears (such as Bosc), peeled, cored and cut into eighths

2 egg whites

4 egg yolks

250 g mascarpone cheese

cocoa powder, for dusting

4 individual serving dishes

serves 6

Line the bottom of each serving dish with sponge fingers, breaking them in order to fit them in.

Put the Marsala or brandy, half of the sugar and 125 ml water in a non-stick frying pan and cook over high heat until the mixture boils, stirring until the sugar has dissolved. Add the pears and cook on a gentle simmer for 20 minutes, turning them often until they are soft and glossy and there is about half of the liquid remaining.

Lay the pears on top of the sponge fingers and pour over the poaching liquid. Using electric beaters, beat the egg whites until firm peaks form. Beat the egg yolks with the remaining sugar for 4–5 minutes, until they are pale in colour and doubled in size, then beat the mascarpone into the yolks until smooth.

Using a large spoon, fold the egg whites into the yolk and sugar mixture and spoon this over the pears. Cover each dish with clingfilm and refrigerate until ready to serve.

Dust each one with a little cocoa powder just before serving.

individual pear, maple & pecan cobblers

4 small ripe pears

finely grated zest and juice of ½ a lemon

4 tablespoons maple syrup

cobbler topping

50 g unsalted butter, chilled

225 g self-raising flour

a pinch of salt

3 tablespoons maple syrup

200 ml milk

50 g roughly chopped pecan nuts

4 individual ovenproof ramekins or similar

a fluted 4–5 cm pastry cutter

serves 4

Preheat the oven to 220°C (425°F) Gas 7.

Peel and core the pears, then slice them thickly lengthwise (or quarter if small and thin). Put the pears into a saucepan with the lemon zest and juice and the maple syrup. Poach gently for 10 minutes until the fruit is almost tender. Set aside.

To make the topping, rub the butter into the flour and salt until it resembles fine breadcrumbs. Stir the maple syrup into the milk and add 150 ml only to the flour, mixing with a blunt knife to form a fairly soft, sticky dough. Tip out onto a flour-dusted work surface and roll out until 2 cm thick. Cut out rounds using the pastry cutter.

Take 4 ramekins and arrange the pear slices around the edge like a star, with the thicker ends in the centre of the dish and the thinner ends pointing upwards out of the dishes. Spoon the juice evenly over the pears and anchor them with a round of cobbler dough placed lightly in the centre. Brush the top of the cobblers with the remaining milk and sprinkle with the chopped nuts. Place the ramekins on a baking tray and bake in the preheated oven for 10–15 minutes, until the cobbler dough is puffed golden brown, and the pears just browning at their tips. Serve hot with double cream or Greek yogurt.

These cheeky little puds will raise a smile as you bring them to the table. Use deep ramekins to achieve the impressive starry effect. They look spectacular – and they taste just as good as they look.

frosted pear, courgette & carrot cake

This is a true celebration of your garden produce, and by packing pears, courgettes and carrots into this cake, you can be sure it will be deliciously moist. Coconut oil often solidifies in its container, so immerse the pot or jar in a bowl of hot water, from the kettle, for about 10 minutes to melt the oil. If you want to make this cake completely dairy-free, replace the butter, cream cheese and yoghurt in the frosting with 200 g soya cream cheese, sweetened with 2 tablespoons icing sugar. This cake will store well for a few days, but even longer if kept in an airtight container in the fridge. Serve it at room temperature.

200 g plain flour

100 g spelt flour

1 slightly rounded teaspoon baking powder

1 teaspoon bicarbonate of soda

1 tablespoon ground cinnamon

2 pinches of ground cloves

4 large eggs

275 g light muscovado or light brown soft sugar

250 ml virgin coconut oil or rapeseed oil

2 medium pears, cored and chopped (no need to peel)

150 g carrots, grated (no need to peel)

100 g courgettes, grated (no need to peel)

100 g sultanas

150 g walnut or pecan pieces

poppy seed frosting

75 g unsalted butter, very soft

200 g cream cheese, chilled

100 g authentic Greek yoghurt, chilled

175 g icing sugar, sifted

1 tablespoon poppy seeds

two 20-cm sandwich tins, 4 cm deep, lightly buttered and base-lined with baking paper

serves 12

Preheat the oven to 180°C (350°F) Gas 4.

Sift the flours, baking powder and bicarbonate of soda into the bowl of an electric mixer (or use a large mixing bowl and an electric whisk). Tip any spelt left in the sieve into the bowl too. Add the cinnamon, cloves, eggs, sugar and oil. Mix together.

In another bowl, mix the pears, carrots, courgettes, sultanas and nuts. Using a large metal spoon, fold these ingredients into the cake mix, making sure everything is thoroughly combined.

Divide the mixture between the prepared tins and spread it evenly with a spatula. Bake in the preheated oven for 40–45 minutes, or until risen, golden and set in the centre. Leave to cool in the tins.

To make the poppy seed frosting, whisk together the butter and cream cheese, add the yoghurt and icing sugar and whisk again – an electric whisk makes quick work of this. Stir in the poppy seeds, then refrigerate until needed.

Tip the cold cakes out of the tins and peel off the base paper. Place one cake on a board or serving plate, bottom-side uppermost. Spread half the frosting over it. Put the other cake on top, top-side uppermost, and spread the remaining frosting over the top.

It's not just apples that go well with pork – if you have plenty of pears, try making this relish to serve with a roast (it also works well with poultry). And if there's fruit left over, preserve it for the winter months. Pickled fruits, such as these delicious pears with tamarind and ginger, can be made with all kinds of vinegars; red and white wine, cider, perry or rice. This recipe uses dark malt vinegar because some varieties of pear turn brown when preserved. The flavour is not impaired, nor the texture of the fruit, but the colour is a little off-putting. If you use dark malt vinegar, the change of colour goes unnoticed. The combination of spices used in this recipe comes originally from the Middle East, but try others such as chilli, dill, allspice or coriander seeds. If you are unable to get hold of tamarind paste, simply omit it.

pickled pears with tamarind & ginger

500 ml malt vinegar (see above)

35 g fresh ginger, peeled and finely grated

3 garlic cloves, crushed

3 heaped teaspoons tamarind paste

1½ teaspoons cumin seeds

a pinch of salt

200 g demerara sugar

1 kg firm pears, peaches, figs or quinces*

3 sealable, sterilized jars, 500 ml each, or a 1.5 litre jar (see note on page 4)

makes 1.5 litres

Put the vinegar, ginger, garlic, tamarind paste, cumin seeds, salt and sugar in a pan and bring slowly to simmering point. Cook over low heat until the sugar has dissolved, then boil for 5 minutes.

Meanwhile, peel the pears, cut in half and pack into the warmed jars. Fill to the brim with the reduced vinegar. If there isn't enough vinegar to cover the fruit, simply boil up extra vinegar, adding 40 g sugar to every 100 ml vinegar, and top up the jars. Seal the jars and label when cold.

Keep at least 3 months before opening. Serve with cheese at the end of a meal, or as part of a cured meat starter, with cold cooked meats, hot gammon, hot game dishes or cold game pies.

*Note Peaches and figs do not need peeling prior to pickling – pears and quinces do.

roasted pear relish

4 ripe pears, peeled, halved and cored

2 tablespoons freshly squeezed lemon juice

1 tablespoon light brown sugar

50 g white granulated sugar

¾ teaspoon ground cinnamon

¼ teaspoon ground cloves

65 ml pure maple syrup

1 small red onion, cut into 1-cm slices

1 tablespoon peeled and grated fresh ginger

5 tablespoons raisins

125 ml cider vinegar

1 teaspoon dried red chilli flakes (optional)

vegetable oil, for brushing

serves 4–6

Preheat the oven to 180°C (350°F) Gas 4.

Brush a baking tray with vegetable oil. In a bowl, combine the pears, lemon juice, both the sugars, cinnamon and cloves and mix well to coat the pears. Arrange the pears cut-side down on the tray and brush with a little more oil. Roast in the preheated oven until caramelized, about 45 minutes. When the pears are cool enough to handle, cut into small cubes.

Meanwhile, put the remaining ingredients in a non-reactive saucepan and bring to the boil. Reduce the heat and simmer, uncovered, for 5 minutes. Remove from the heat and leave to cool. Add the cubed pears to the onion mixture and mix well. Cover and refrigerate for at least 1 day before serving. Transfer the relish to a spotlessly clean and dry, sealable airtight container. It will keep in the fridge for up to 10 days.

warm pear, gorgonzola & pecan tartlets with maple drizzle

375 g ready-rolled puff pastry
1 egg, lightly beaten
200 g Gorgonzola
4 tablespoons double cream
cayenne pepper

75 g shelled pecan nuts
or walnuts
2–3 ripe pears
6 teaspoons maple syrup

serves 6

Preheat the oven to 220°C (425°F) Gas 7.

Take the pastry out of the fridge and leave to warm up a little for 10–15 minutes.

Unroll the pastry, cut it in half horizontally, then cut each of the halves into 3 to make 6 equal-sized pieces. With the tip of a sharp knife, score round each of the squares about 1.5 cm from the edge to make a border. Lightly brush the border with beaten egg, taking care not to brush over the cut you've made (otherwise the pastry won't puff up around the edge of the tartlets).

Put the Gorgonzola in a bowl and break up roughly with a fork, then stir in the cream. Season with a little cayenne pepper and spread over the bases of the tartlets, taking care not to cover the border. Roughly break up the pecan nuts and divide between the tartlets. Peel, core and quarter the pears, cut each quarter into 3 wedges and lay them in overlapping slices on top of the cheese and nuts. Drizzle a teaspoonful of maple syrup over each tart and bake in the preheated oven for 15–20 minutes until the pastry is well browned and puffed up. Leave to cool for 5 minutes before serving.

Pears have a natural affinity with blue cheese and are a classic combination, especially with walnuts added too. These mouth-watering golden tartlets are a cheese course and dessert rolled into one – a fabulous finale for a dinner party.

Here are sweet, sticky plum fudge puddings and a comforting crumble that is cooked under the grill. Plum crumble is a classic, but you could use any fruit you have – just be aware that soft summer berries will need very little time in the pan, while apples and pears will require a little longer.

pan plum crumble

185 ml freshly squeezed orange juice

2 tablespoons caster sugar

6 ripe plums, halved and stoned

100 g self-raising flour

60 g soft brown sugar

60 g porridge oats

50 g unsalted butter, cubed and chilled

vanilla ice cream, to serve

serves 4–6

Put the orange juice and caster sugar in a small frying pan and set it over high heat. Bring the mixture to the boil, then reduce the heat to medium. Add the plums, cut-side down, and cook for 5 minutes. Turn the plums over and cook for a further 5 minutes, until they have softened yet still retain their shape and the liquid has almost evaporated. Remove the pan from the heat and set aside.

Preheat the grill to medium.

Put the flour, brown sugar and oats in a bowl and mix just to combine. Add the butter and use your fingertips to rub it into the dry ingredients.

Sprinkle the mixture evenly over the plums and slide the frying pan under the hot grill for 2–3 minutes, until the crumble is golden. Serve warm with a scoop of vanilla ice cream.

plum fudge puddings

50 g unsalted butter

50 g honey

2 tablespoons double cream

2 tablespoons soft brown sugar

1 teaspoon ground mixed spice

75 g fresh white breadcrumbs

2 ripe plums, halved, stoned and thinly sliced

crème fraîche, to serve

4 ramekins, 150 ml each

serves 4

Put the butter, honey and cream into a saucepan and heat until melted. Put the sugar, spice and breadcrumbs into a bowl and mix thoroughly.

Divide half the buttery fudge mixture between the ramekin dishes and top with a layer of plum slices and half the breadcrumb mix. Add the remaining plums and breadcrumbs, then spoon over the remaining sauce.

Set the ramekins on a baking tray and bake in a preheated oven at 200°C (400°F) Gas 6 for 20 minutes. Remove from the oven and leave to cool for 5 minutes, then carefully unmould the puddings and serve with a spoonful of crème fraîche.

greengage jam

1.5 kg greengages or other plums

1 large whole star anise

1.5 kg sugar

2–4 clean, sealable, sterilized jars, 250 g each

makes 500 g–1 kg

Rinse the fruit, remove the stalks and let dry naturally in the sun. Put the fruit in a large saucepan with the star anise and 100 ml water and simmer gently to soften the skins, taking care not to let the fruit become mushy.

Discard the star anise. Add the sugar and continue to simmer over low heat to dissolve the sugar, stirring all the time. Bring to the boil and remove as many stones as come to the surface. Boil rapidly until setting point is reached (see page 166), 5–10 minutes.

If the jam is not ready, put the pan back on the heat to boil for a few minutes longer and test again. Repeat this process if necessary and remember to take the jam off the heat while testing, because over-boiling will ruin it.

When setting point has been reached, skim the jam with a perforated skimmer, stir it well and let stand for 20 minutes for the fruit to settle. Stir and ladle into jars. Seal at once with waxed paper discs and close with a lid or appropriate cover.

Let cool, label and store in a cool, dark cupboard until required.

Variation Victoria Plum Jam

If using large plum varieties such as Victoria, it may be a good idea to cut the plums in half and remove the stones before cooking.

Greengage jam is an English country classic, and the perfect way to savour a bumper crop. Plum and aniseed makes a wonderful combination, whether for jam, chutney, bottling, stewing, pies, crumbles or fools. Cinnamon and cloves also work well if aniseed is not a favourite of yours, but do try it first. Greengages make a dark golden-yellow jam, but you can use other plum varieties to make jams that vary in colour from yellow to pink or purple. If you grow a sweet plum variety, they can also be used to bake this irresistible plum tart, perfectly combined with sharp, strongly flavoured apples. This one has plenty of fruit filling, which makes it wonderfully juicy.

plum & apple tart

45 g unsalted butter, at room temperature

90 g golden caster sugar

1 egg

1½ teaspoons baking powder

90 g plain flour

375 g ready-rolled sweet shortcrust pastry, defrosted if frozen

10 Victoria plums, pitted and halved

2 Bramley apples, cored and sliced

3 tablespoons apricot jam, to glaze (optional)

a 23-cm loose-based fluted tart tin, greased

makes about 8 slices

Preheat the oven to 160°C (325°F) Gas 3.

To make the cake mixture, put the butter and sugar in a mixing bowl and mix with an electric whisk to combine. Mix in the egg and baking powder with the whisk, then gently fold in the flour by hand until evenly combined.

Line the tart tin with the shortcrust pastry and trim the excess dough neatly around the edges. Spoon the cake mixture into the tart shell and spread evenly. Scatter the plums and apples all over the mixture.

Bake in the preheated oven for 40 minutes. When the tart is ready, the fruit will have sunk a little and the cake will have risen up in parts and be golden. Remove from the oven and leave to cool for a few minutes.

In the meantime, put the apricot jam, if using, in a small saucepan and heat gently until melted and runny. Brush the jam all over the tart filling with a pastry brush and leave for a few more minutes before serving. Alternatively, serve it chilled with cream or custard.

When peaches are in season and at their juicy best, the most simple of recipes are all that are required to bring out the best of the fruit. This rustic tart is so easy (you don't even need a tin) and so tasty. Or simply roast the peaches in the oven and serve them with lashings of indulgent mascarpone cheese. The vanilla sugar is easy to make – just put a couple of vanilla pods in a jar of sugar and leave them there, topping up with fresh sugar as necessary.

free-form caramelized peach tart

375 g ready-made puff pastry, defrosted if frozen

4–6 ripe peaches

55 g butter

freshly squeezed juice of ½ lemon

150 g caster sugar

whipped cream or crème fraîche, to serve

a dinner plate, 28 cm diameter (to use as a template)

a baking tray

serves 6

Preheat the oven to 230°C (450°F) Gas 8.

Roll out the pastry on a lightly floured work surface and cut out a circle, 28 cm diameter, using a large dinner plate as a template. Lift onto a baking tray and make an edge by twisting the pastry over itself all the way around the edge. Press lightly to seal. Still on the baking tray, chill or freeze for at least 15 minutes.

Peel the peaches if necessary, then halve and stone them and cut into chunky slices. Put the butter into a saucepan, then add the lemon juice and half the sugar. Heat until melted, then add the peaches and toss gently. Pile the peaches all over the pastry in a casual way. Sprinkle with the remaining sugar and bake in the preheated oven for 20–25 minutes until golden, puffed and caramelized. Serve with whipped cream or crème fraîche.

roasted mascarpone peaches

4 large ripe peaches

2 tablespoons clear honey

150 g mascarpone cheese

3 tablespoons vanilla sugar

1 tablespoon freshly squeezed lemon juice

serves 4

Cut the peaches in half, remove the stones and arrange the fruit cut side up in a roasting tin. Pour over the honey and bake in a preheated oven at 200°C (400°F) Gas 6 for about 20 minutes until softened and lightly golden.

Mix the mascarpone with the vanilla sugar and lemon juice and spoon onto the hot peaches. Serve at once.

If you have an abundance of juicy summer peaches, try these two recipes: a cake to enjoy straight away, and a jar of preserved fruit to store in the cupboard and bring out for a quick dessert, served with cream. You can use either yellow or white peaches here – the yellow varieties have a more robust flavour, while the white ones are more subtle. Peach halves in brandy are a classic, but all kinds of fruits can be preserved in this way: try nectarine halves, cherries, apricots, or plums (although these fruits will not need to be peeled) and substitute the star anise for a cinnamon stick or vanilla pod.

peach halves in brandy with star anise

4 firm just-ripe peaches
400 g sugar
200 ml brandy
1 whole star anise

1 x 500 ml sterilized, sealable jar (see note on page 4)

makes 500 ml

Put the peaches in a large bowl and cover with boiling water. Leave for 2 minutes for the skins to lift, drain off the water and pull off the skins. Discard the water. Cut the peaches in half and poach in plenty of simmering water for 1–2 minutes until just tender. Lift out the peach halves with a slotted spoon and drain on kitchen paper.

Measure 500 ml of the poaching water into a pan. Add 300 g of the sugar, dissolve over low heat, then bring to the boil and boil for 7 minutes. Don't forget to keep an eye on it.

When the peaches have cooled, arrange them in a heatproof dish in a single layer, cover with the boiling syrup and leave for 24 hours.

After this time, pour the syrup off the peach halves into a saucepan and add the remaining 100 g sugar. Bring slowly to simmering point to dissolve the sugar, then boil for 2 minutes. Pour this back over the peaches, cool, cover with a cloth or lid and leave for 2 more days. After 2 days, transfer the peach halves to a clean 500 ml jar.

Pour 200 ml of the syrup into a measuring jug and add to it an equal quantity of brandy. Pour the mixture over the peaches until covered, add the star anise on the outside of the fruit but on the inside of the glass and keep for at least 1 month before using.

upside-down peach cake

4 large peaches
125 g unsalted butter, softened
185 g soft brown sugar
3 eggs, separated
185 g self-raising flour
250 g soured cream

icing sugar, for dusting
single cream, to serve (optional)

a 23-cm diameter springform cake tin, base-lined with baking paper and lightly greased

Preheat the oven to 180°C (350°F) Gas 4. Halve the peaches, discard the stone, then cut each half in half again. Arrange the peach quarters on the bottom of the cake tin and set aside while making the cake mixture.

Put the butter and sugar in a large bowl and beat with an electric whisk until the sugar has completely dissolved and the mixture is the colour of caramel. Add the egg yolks, 1 at a time, beating for 1 minute between each addition. Fold the flour and soured cream through in 2 batches.

In a separate grease-free bowl, beat the egg whites with an electric whisk until they form firm peaks. Using a large metal spoon, fold the whites into the cake mixture in 2 batches. Spoon the mixture over the peaches and bake in the preheated oven for 40–45 minutes, until the top of the cake is golden and the centre springs back when gently pressed.

Let cool in the tin for 10 minutes before carefully turning out onto a serving plate. Dust with icing sugar and serve warm with single cream for pouring, if liked.

These two summery recipes are packed full of sweet, ripe produce. The nectarines in both recipes can be swapped for a similar quantity of peaches, plums or apricots, to suit your crop. But whatever fruit you choose, the tray bake is best made and eaten on the same day. Crumbles are normally considered to be a comforting winter pudding, but this deliciously light, nutty version makes the most of juicy summer nectarines. It takes very little time to prepare and tastes sublime with ice cream.

nectarine, blueberry & lavender tray bake

3 large eggs
200 g caster sugar
175 g self-raising flour, sifted
1 teaspoon baking powder
½ teaspoon vanilla extract
175 g butter, softened and cubed
½ tablespoon dried lavender buds
3 ripe but firm nectarines
200 g blueberries
1 tablespoon polenta

lavender sugar
½ tablespoon dried lavender buds
2 tablespoons caster sugar
grated zest of 1 unwaxed lemon

a 20 x 33-cm baking tin, 3–4 cm deep, lined with baking paper and lightly buttered

serves 14

Preheat the oven to 180°C (350°F) Gas 4.

Put the eggs, sugar, flour, baking powder, vanilla extract, butter and lavender in an electric mixer (or use a mixing bowl and an electric whisk) and whisk together. Stone the nectarines, chop them into bite-sized pieces and stir into the mixture along with the blueberries.

Dust the bottom of the prepared tin with the polenta and a very small amount of flour. Spoon the mixture into the tin and spread it evenly with a spatula.

To make the lavender sugar, mix all the ingredients together in a bowl, then scatter evenly over the tray bake.

Bake in the preheated oven for 35 minutes, or until risen and golden brown. Leave to cool in the tin before cutting into 14 rectangles.

nectarine & pistachio summer crumble

70 g whole pistachio nuts, coarsely chopped
50 g blanched whole almonds
60 g ground oatmeal
50 g cold unsalted butter, cubed
60 g plain flour
50 g soft brown sugar

6 nectarines
vanilla ice cream or double cream, to serve

a baking tray, lined with baking paper

serves 6

To make the crumble topping, put the pistachios and almonds in a food processor and process until coarsely chopped. Transfer to a bowl. Add the oatmeal and butter and use your fingertips to rub the ingredients together until the mixture resembles coarse, wet sand. Add the flour and sugar and rub together to combine. Cover and refrigerate until needed.

Preheat the oven to 220°C (425°F) Gas 7.

Line a baking tray with baking paper. Cut the nectarines in half. If the stone does not come out easily, don't worry – simply slice the flesh off the fruit and drop it directly onto the baking tray. Sprinkle the crumble topping evenly over the nectarines and bake in the preheated oven for 10–15 minutes, until the fruit is soft and juicy and the topping is a soft golden colour. Serve warm with ice cream or double cream.

The word slump perfectly describes the sloppy batter which covers the seasonal fruit in this satisfying pudding. Normally the fruit is on the bottom and the thick batter spooned or poured roughly over the top but this recipe celebrates the fruit, so pour the batter in first, then push in the apricots. You can use any juicy fruit and berries are really good too. The apricot betty is another wonderful, old-fashioned fruit pudding. If you have the patience, you can crack the apricot kernels and take out the nuts inside. These are very like bitter almonds, and are a fantastic addition when chopped and toasted with the breadcrumbs.

buttered apricot betty

675 g fresh apricots

100 g unsalted butter, diced

150 g fresh breadcrumbs, lightly toasted

2 tablespoons golden syrup

100 ml orange juice

50 g caster sugar

a medium, ovenproof, deep pie or soufflé dish

a large roasting tin

serves 4

Preheat the oven to 190°C (375°F) Gas 5.

Halve the fresh apricots and remove the stones. Butter a deep pie or soufflé dish and place a layer of apricots on the base.

Reserve 4–6 tablespoons of breadcrumbs for the top. Sprinkle some of the rest of the breadcrumbs over the apricots, and dot with some of the butter. Put in some more apricots and repeat these alternate casual layers until all the apricots and breadcrumbs are used up. Use the reserved breadcrumbs for the final top layer.

Warm the syrup with the orange juice, and pour this over the top. Sprinkle with sugar and dot with the remaining butter.

Place the pie dish in a roasting tin and pour in enough boiling water to come halfway up the sides of the dish. Bake in the preheated oven for 45 minutes, or until the apricots are soft and the top crispy and golden brown. Serve warm, not hot, with cream.

apricot & almond slump

600 g fresh apricots

150 g golden caster sugar

almond slump batter

200 g plain flour

3 teaspoons baking powder

a pinch of salt

100 g ground almonds

about 350 ml milk

4 tablespoons unsalted butter, melted

30 g whole blanched almonds

a large, non-stick, metal baking tin

serves 4–6

Preheat the oven to 190°C (375°F) Gas 5.

Halve the apricots, remove the stones and mix with 100 g of the sugar. Set aside until needed.

Sift together the flour, baking powder, salt and remaining 50 g of sugar into a bowl. Stir in the ground almonds, the milk and melted butter and whisk until smooth and thick. Pour the batter into a lightly buttered tin, then push in the apricots cut side up, but in a higgledy-piggledy manner and slightly at an angle all over. Place a whole almond inside each apricot where the stone once was.

Bake the slump for 25–30 minutes in the middle of the preheated oven, until risen and golden.

Remove from the oven and allow to cool slightly before serving with vanilla ice cream.

white chocolate & apricot roulade

This summer stunner, once assembled, will hold for a couple of hours before serving – keep it in a cool place, but not the fridge. To make it look extra special, use a vegetable peeler to make curls from a block of white chocolate to scatter on top.

Preheat the oven to 190°C (375°F) Gas 5.

Break the eggs into a large heatproof mixing bowl and add the sugar and saffron. Place over a pan of simmering water, making sure the base doesn't touch the water. Using an electric whisk, whisk the ingredients for 5 minutes, or until pale and voluminous. Take the bowl off the heat. Using a large metal spoon, carefully fold the flour into the mixture.

Tip the mixture into the prepared tin and gently spread it evenly with a spatula. Sprinkle the flaked almonds over the top. Bake in the preheated oven for 12–15 minutes, or until lightly golden. Meanwhile, cover a large board with a sheet of baking paper and sift the tablespoon of icing sugar evenly over it.

When the sponge is ready, remove from the oven and leave it to settle for 10 minutes. Run a small, sharp knife around the edges before turning it upside down over the sugared baking paper. Remove the tin and peel off the base paper. Roll up the sponge from one of the shorter ends, rolling the sugared baking paper with it as you do so – you may need to make a cut along the width of the sponge a couple of centimetres in, to help you start rolling. Once rolled, leave the sponge to cool completely.

To make the apricot filling, put all the ingredients in a pan and simmer gently, uncovered, for 10 minutes – you want the apricots to be soft, but still retain their shape. Leave to cool, then refrigerate until needed.

To make the white chocolate cream, put the chocolate pieces and 2 tablespoons of the crème fraîche in a small heatproof bowl over a pan of barely simmering water. Leave until melted, stirring from time to time. Take the bowl off the heat and leave to cool slightly. Whisk the cream in a bowl until it forms soft peaks, then stir in the remaining crème fraîche and the cooled chocolate mixture.

Unroll the sponge onto a large board. Spread the white chocolate cream over it and scatter the apricot mixture on top. Roll up the roulade and dust with icing sugar.

4 large eggs

100 g caster sugar

2 pinches of saffron threads

100 g self-raising flour, sifted

3 tablespoons flaked almonds

1 tablespoon icing sugar, plus extra for dusting

apricot filling

seeds from 4 cardamom pods, crushed

1 tablespoon orange blossom honey or other runny honey

1 tablespoon freshly squeezed lemon juice

8 apricots, stoned and finely chopped

white chocolate cream

75 g white chocolate, broken into pieces, plus extra if making curls

175 g crème fraîche

200 ml double cream

a 24 x 37-cm Swiss roll tin, 2.5 cm deep, oiled and base lined with baking paper

serves 10–12

apricots 163

cherry, peach & vanilla shortcake

100 g plain flour

75 g butter, softened and cubed

40 g icing sugar, sifted

1 egg yolk

topping

1 vanilla pod, split lengthways

125 ml double or whipping cream, chilled

2 tablespoons icing sugar, plus extra for dusting

2 ripe but firm peaches, stoned and sliced

100 g cherries, stoned and halved

a squeeze of lemon juice

2 tablespoons freshly shredded basil leaves

a baking tray, lined with baking paper

serves 4

This is such a pretty option for a summer afternoon tea in the garden, but it can also be adapted to whatever seasonal fruits are available. Strawberries and raspberries make a nice topping with a little shredded lemon verbena, or try thin slices of baked quince, a handful of blackberries and a scattering of toasted nuts for a wonderful autumn variation.

Put the flour, butter, sugar and egg yolk in a food processor and mix together. If the dough doesn't come together, tip it into a bowl and work it with a spatula. Alternatively, you can make it by hand to start with. Tip the dough onto a lightly floured work surface and bring it together in a ball. Press the ball into a disc, wrap in clingfilm and refrigerate for 15 minutes.

Preheat the oven to 190°C (375°F) Gas 5.

Tip the dough out onto the lightly floured surface and roll or pat it out until it is big enough to cut out a 15-cm round – you can use a plate or upturned bowl to cut around.

Transfer the round to the prepared baking tray and bake in the preheated oven for 10–12 minutes, or until set and lightly golden at the edges. Leave to cool completely.

To make the topping, scrape the seeds out of the vanilla pod into a bowl with the cream and half the icing sugar. Whip into soft peaks.

Toss the sliced peaches and halved cherries with the lemon juice, basil and the remaining icing sugar.

Dust the cold shortcake lightly with more icing sugar, then top with the cream mixture and scatter the fruit mixture over the top. Serve immediately.

Who said summer cooking couldn't include comfort food? These hearty baked desserts include a classic French clafoutis, and a modern take on a retro strudel. Fresh ricotta cheese is combined with summer-ripe cherries and crispy filo with great success.

cherry & ricotta strudel

500 g fresh cherries, stoned

60 g icing sugar, plus extra for dusting

2 teaspoons cornflour

100 g ground almonds*

150 g fresh ricotta cheese

8 sheets of filo pastry, thawed if frozen

75 g unsalted butter, melted

serves 8

Put the cherries, 1 tablespoon of the icing sugar and the cornflour in a bowl and let sit for 30 minutes, stirring often. Preheat the oven to 220°C (425°F) Gas 7.

Put the ground almonds and 2 tablepoons of the remaining icing sugar in a bowl and mix to combine. Put the ricotta in a separate bowl, add the remaining icing sugar and mix to combine. Set aside until needed. Put a baking tray in the preheated oven to heat up. (This will prevent the bottom of the filo becoming soggy.)

Put a sheet of baking paper on a work surface. Lay a sheet of filo on the baking paper, longest edge nearest to you. Brush all over with melted butter until the filo is shiny. Sprinkle 1–2 tablespoons of the ground almond mixture over the pastry. Repeat with the remaining sheets of filo, butter and almond mixture, finishing with the final sheet of filo.

Working quickly, so that the filo does not become soggy, spread the ricotta mixture over the pastry, leaving a 5-cm margin around the edges. Spoon the cherry mixture over the top. Fold the edge nearest to you up and over the filling, tucking in the shorter edges as you roll. Make sure the strudel is sitting seam-side down. Use the baking paper to lift the strudel onto the hot baking tray. Bake in the preheated oven for 12–15 minutes, until lightly golden.

Remove and allow to cool slightly before dusting liberally with icing sugar and cutting into slices to serve.

*Note You can buy pre-packed ground almonds, or grind your own. It only takes a few minutes and the difference in fuller, richer flavour is well worth it. Simply put them on a baking tray and toast them in an oven preheated to 180°C (350°F) Gas 4 for 5 minutes. Allow them to cool and then process them in a food processor.

cherry & almond clafoutis

100 g blanched almonds

1 vanilla pod (optional)

3 tablespoons plain flour

225 g caster sugar

4 eggs

2 egg yolks

250 ml single cream

250 g cherries, torn in half and stoned

a round ovenproof dish, 20–23 cm diameter

serves 4

Preheat the oven to 220°C (425°F) Gas 7.

Put the almonds on a baking tray and toast them in the preheated oven for 6–8 minutes, until lightly golden. Remove and leave to cool. Put the cooled almonds in a food processor and process until they resemble a coarse meal. Scrape the seeds from the vanilla pod into the food processor with the almonds and process until the mixture resembles a coarse meal. Add the flour and sugar and process to mix. Add the eggs, egg yolks and cream and process again until you have a smooth, thick batter. Transfer to a bowl, cover and refrigerate until needed – it will keep for 2 days in the refrigerator.

Put the torn cherry halves in the bottom of an ovenproof dish. Carefully pour the batter over the cherries. If need be, rearrange the cherries to evenly distribute. (If using refrigerated batter, beat it until well mixed before pouring over the cherries.)

Cook in the preheated oven for 25 minutes, until the clafoutis is puffed up and golden brown. Allow to cool for a few minutes before serving. The clafoutis will sink during this time. Serve the clafoutis hot with vanilla ice cream.

italian fig conserve

1.5 kg firm black figs
freshly squeezed juice
of 2 lemons
1.2 kg sugar
1 envelope of vanilla sugar,
7.5 g (optional)

*3–4 sealable, sterilized jars
(see note on page 4)
waxed paper discs*

makes 750 g–1 kg

Wipe the figs and chop into tiny pieces. Put in a saucepan with the lemon juice and 200 ml water. Cook over low heat until soft – this may take 20–30 minutes, but if the skins are not cooked until tender at this stage, they will be tough when boiled with the sugar. Add the sugar and cook over low heat until dissolved. Stir in the vanilla sugar, increase the heat and boil until setting point is reached, about 5–10 minutes.

Take the pan off the heat and test for set. If the jam is not ready, put the pan back on the heat to boil for a few minutes longer and test again. Repeat this process if necessary and remember to take the jam off the heat while testing, because over-boiling will ruin it.

When the jam has reached setting point, skim it with a perforated skimmer, stir it well and let stand for 20 minutes for the fruit to settle. Stir and ladle into clean, dry, warm jars. Seal at once with waxed paper discs, wiping the necks of the jars with a clean, damp cloth if necessary. Close with a lid or appropriate cover. Leave to cool, label and store in a cool, dark cupboard until required.

Variation Try experimenting with peaches, nectarines and kiwifruit, though it may not be necessary to cook the fruit for so long.

Although ripe figs are delicious enjoyed as they are, cooking them really brings out the sweetness. To make this delicious fig conserve, make sure you use only plump, firm fruit. You can use green figs, but they should be peeled first. It is perfect with crusty bread and butter, brioche or toast for breakfast, but would also make excellent jam tartlets.

✳ tip

This is a simple method for testing the setting point of jam without the aid of a sugar thermometer. As the jam boils it will start to become thicker and more syrupy. At this point, take it off the heat and put a teaspoonful on a saucer that you have chilled in the fridge. Leave for 5 minutes, the push the surface of the jam with your finger – if it wrinkles, the jam has reached setting point, otherwise return to the heat and boil again, testing at 4–5 minute intervals.

Muscat is a grape variety that produces deliciously sweet and syrupy dessert wines known as moscato in Italy and moscatel in Spain. Whichever one you choose, the result will be the same – a fragrant and light dessert that is guaranteed to delight.

spiced muscat figs

250 ml muscat (sweet dessert wine)

125 g caster sugar

1 vanilla pod

2 cardamom pods, lightly crushed

2 strips of orange zest

8 fresh green figs

serves 4

Put the muscat, sugar, vanilla and cardamom pods and orange zest in a medium saucepan and set over high heat. Bring the mixture to the boil, then reduce the heat to medium. Add the figs to the pan, cover and cook for 20–25 minutes, until the figs are very tender. Remove the figs from the pan with a slotted spoon and set aside.

Return the liquid to the boil and cook for 8–10 minutes, until thick and syrupy.

Serve 2 figs per person, with the syrup spooned over the top.

soft fruits

strawberry tiramisú ❧ pink cava & strawberry jellies

strawberry buttermilk cake

summer fruit & white chocolate muffins

strawberry jam ❧ strawberries with black pepper

chocolate-dipped strawberries ❧ strawberry eton mess

fresh raspberry & almond tart ❧ little raspberry &

rose cobblers ❧ **uncooked freezer raspberry jam**

raspberry cream ❧ **blackberry crumble**

baked brioche pudding with blackberries

baked granny smith & blueberry pudding

cinnamon blueberry cake ❧ **rhubarb clafoutis**

rhubarb, strawberry & rose fool

rhubarb custard & crumble tartlets

Here are two fruity desserts that are sure to delight guests at a summer garden party. A sumptuous Italian classic has been given a summer makeover with the inclusion of freshly picked strawberries. And, on the lighter side, pink cava and strawberry jellies make a delicate, pretty dessert. Adding a dash of strawberry-flavoured syrup or liqueur to the liquid jelly will make this even more delicious.

strawberry tiramisù

400 g fresh ripe strawberries

5 hard amaretti biscuits

2 large eggs, separated

40 g unrefined caster sugar

¼ teaspoon vanilla extract

4 tablespoons white rum

250 g mascarpone cheese, at room temperature

3 tablespoons whipping cream

100 ml pressed apple juice

½ 200-g pack savoiardi (sponge finger biscuits)

a medium–large, deep, glass dessert bowl

serves 6

Hull the strawberries. Weigh out 100 g and chop them finely. Slice the remaining strawberries and set aside. Put the amaretti biscuits in a plastic bag, seal, then hit them with a rolling pin until they are the consistency of coarse breadcrumbs.

Beat the egg yolks in a bowl with an electric handheld whisk or a whisk until pale yellow and fluffy, gradually adding the sugar as you go. Add the vanilla extract and a tablespoon of the white rum. Tip the mascarpone cheese into a large bowl, beat with a wooden spoon to soften, then gradually add the egg yolk mixture and beat until smooth. In another bowl, whisk the egg whites until they just hold a soft peak. Fold the chopped strawberries into the mascarpone cheese mixture, then carefully fold in the egg whites.

Whip the cream to a similar consistency then fold that in too, along with a third of the crushed amaretti biscuits. Mix the remaining rum with the apple juice. Dip some of the savoiardi in the apple-rum mixture and lay across the base of your bowl. Reserving some sliced strawberries for decoration, arrange a layer of strawberries over the biscuits, then cover with a layer of mascarpone cream. Repeat with 1 or 2 more layers of soaked biscuits, strawberries and mascarpone cream, finishing with the mascarpone cream. Cover the bowl tightly with clingfilm and chill for at least 5 hours.

About 1 hour before serving, sprinkle the remaining amaretti biscuits over the top of the tiramisù, then decorate with the remaining strawberries. Return the tiramisù to the refrigerator until you are ready to serve it.

pink cava & strawberry jellies

12 sheets of gelatine (or enough to set 1.1 litres of liquid)

1.1 litres Cava Rosado or other sparkling rosé

800 g fresh strawberries

2–3 tablespoons caster sugar, depending on how ripe your strawberries are

90–125 ml homemade sugar syrup* or shop-bought gomme

cream or vanilla ice cream, to serve

12 wine glasses or small glass serving dishes

serves 12

Lay the gelatine in a large flat dish and sprinkle over 6 tablespoons cold water. Leave to soak for 3 minutes until soft. Heat the wine in a microwave or saucepan until hot but not boiling. Tip the soaked gelatine into the wine and stir to dissolve, then set aside to cool.

Rinse the strawberries, cut them into halves or quarters to give even-sized pieces and put them into a shallow bowl, sprinkle over the sugar and leave them to macerate. Check the liquid jelly for sweetness, adding the sugar syrup to taste. Divide half the strawberries between 12 glasses or glass dishes then pour over enough jelly to cover them. Put in the fridge to chill. As soon as the jelly has set (about an hour), add the rest of the fruit and jelly. Return to the fridge to set for another 45 minutes–1 hour before serving with cream or ice cream.

*Note To make the sugar syrup, dissolve 125 g sugar in 150 ml water. Heat gently together in a pan. When all the grains are dissolved, bring to the boil and simmer for 2–3 minutes. Use it immediately or cool and store it for up to two weeks in the refrigerator.

strawberries 173

Sweet summer strawberries are so good you will want to eat a whole bowl on their own. Although strawberries are a fruit that are best appreciated raw, occasionally you will come across great recipes to the contrary, like these two: a smooth, dense cake given a light and creamy crumb by using buttermilk, or moist muffins packed full of fruit and nuggets of white chocolate. Both are a truly indulgent treat.

summer fruit & white chocolate muffins

2 eggs	topping
80 g golden caster sugar	30 g nectarine, stoned and sliced
50 ml vegetable oil (or groundnut or sunflower)	60 g raspberries
a few drops of vanilla extract	30 g strawberries, hulled and quartered
150 g plain flour	light brown soft sugar, to sprinkle
1½ teaspoons baking powder	
1 large nectarine, stoned and sliced	*a muffin tray, lined with 6 large muffin cases*
70 g strawberries, hulled and quartered	**makes 6**
70 g white chocolate, chopped	

Preheat the oven to 180ºC (350ºF) Gas 4.

Put the eggs, sugar, oil and vanilla in a mixing bowl and mix well until you have a smooth liquid. Mix the flour and baking powder together in a separate bowl, then mix into the wet ingredients. Stir in the nectarines, strawberries and chocolate until evenly mixed.

Fill each muffin case about two-thirds full with batter. Scatter the fruit for the topping over the muffins and finish with a sprinkling of sugar. Bake in the preheated oven for about 25 minutes. Do not be tempted to open the oven door halfway through baking as it might cause the muffins to sink. When they are ready, they should be well risen and springy to the touch.

Muffins are always best eaten warm from the oven, but if you have some left over you can always refresh them with a quick flash in the microwave. Store in an airtight container for 2–3 days.

strawberry buttermilk cake

250 g self-raising flour	**crumble topping**
225 g caster sugar	40 g plain flour
125 g unsalted butter, softened	50 g unsalted butter, chilled and cubed
2 eggs	95 g soft brown sugar
225 ml buttermilk	
375 g strawberries, hulled, large ones halved	*a 24 cm x 24 cm cake tin, greased and lined*
vanilla custard or double cream, to serve	**serves 6–8**

Preheat the oven to 180ºC (350ºF) Gas 4.

Put the flour and sugar in a bowl and mix. Put the butter, eggs and buttermilk in a food processor and process until smooth and combined. With the motor running, add the flour and sugar and process until well mixed. Scrape down the sides of the bowl to evenly incorporate all the ingredients. Transfer the mixture to a bowl and stir in the strawberries. Spoon the batter into the lined cake tin.

To make the crumble topping, put the flour and butter in a bowl and, using the tips of your fingers, rub the butter into the flour until the mixture resembles coarse breadcrumbs. Stir in the sugar.

Evenly sprinkle the topping mixture over the cake and bake in the preheated oven for 50 minutes, until golden brown on top.

Leave to cool before cutting into slices or squares and serving with vanilla custard or a dollop of double cream.

strawberry jam

900 g slightly under-ripe strawberries, hulled and halved

750 g preserving or granulated sugar

freshly squeezed juice of 1 lemon

10 g butter

2 x 325-ml sealable, sterilized jars (see note on page 4)

waxed paper discs

makes 2 x 325-ml jars

Put the strawberries and sugar in a large non-metal bowl. Cover and leave to macerate overnight.

The next day, transfer the contents of the bowl to a large preserving pan or non-aluminium saucepan and set over very low heat to dissolve any remaining sugar. Add the lemon juice and bring to the boil. Cook for 8–25 minutes, depending on the water content of the strawberries, or until setting point has been reached (for tips to test for set, see page 166).

Stir in the butter to disperse any scum. Leave to cool for about 20 minutes, then transfer to the sterilized jars (wiping off any drips). Cover with waxed discs and seal with the lids whilst still warm. Label with the date and store in a cool, dark place for up to 6 months.

strawberries with black pepper

500 g strawberries

1 tablespoon orange flower water (optional)

1 tablespoon caster sugar

2 teaspoons cracked black pepper

serves 4

Hull the strawberries and cut in half. Sprinkle with the orange flower water, if using, and with the sugar and black pepper. Chill for 15 minutes and serve.

Note Strawberries should be washed and dried before hulling, not after, otherwise they fill up with water.

chocolate-dipped strawberries

100 g dark chocolate

100 g white chocolate

12 large strawberries

baking paper

12 wooden skewers

serves 12

Put the chocolate into 2 separate bowls and set the bowls over 2 saucepans of simmering water. When melted, dip the pointed end of each strawberry into one of the chocolates and transfer to the sheet of baking paper. When set, slide each strawberry onto a skewer and serve.

strawberry eton mess

300 ml double (or whipping) cream

200 g thick Greek-style yoghurt

6 plain meringues or meringue shells

16 ripe, juicy strawberries, halved

serves 4–6

Put the cream into a large bowl whisk until it makes soft peaks. Don't over-whisk otherwise the cream will be too firm. Add the yoghurt and gently fold everything together.

Over another bowl, gently crush the meringues with your fingers to break into small pieces. Add the meringue and strawberries to the cream mixture and gently mix together.

Spoon the mixture into small bowls and put in the fridge for 20 minutes before you serve.

If you have an abundance of raspberries, they freeze really well and can be used in future dishes. These two recipes use frozen raspberries, as they are often easier to work with when a little less mushy. The raspberry and almond tart tastes better the day after it's made, which makes it ideal for preparing ahead of any guests arriving for a summer afternoon tea!

fresh raspberry & almond tart

1 egg

3 tablespoons caster sugar

1 tablespoon plain flour

75 g unsalted butter

150 g fresh raspberries, frozen until firm

chilled cream, to serve (optional)

almond shortcrust pastry

50 g ground almonds

200 g plain flour

80 g caster sugar

125 g unsalted butter, chilled and cubed

a rectangular tart tin, 37 x 10 cm, lightly greased

serves 6–8

Preheat the oven to 180°C (350°F) Gas 4.

To make the pastry, put the ground almonds, flour and sugar in a food processor. With the motor running, add a cube of butter at a time until it is all incorporated and the mixture resembles coarse breadcrumbs. Add 2 tablespoons cold water and process until just combined. Be careful not to overprocess.

Tip the pastry out onto a lightly-floured work surface and knead to form a ball. Roll it out between 2 layers of baking paper until it is about 5 cm longer and 5 cm wider than the tart tin. Carefully lift the pastry into the tin and use your fingers to press it down into the base and sides, letting it overhang. Prick the base all over with a fork and bake in the preheated oven for 20 minutes, until lightly golden. Break off the overhanging pastry.

Put the egg, sugar and flour in a bowl and use a balloon whisk to beat until thick and pale. Put the butter in a small saucepan and set over medium heat. Let melt until frothy and dark golden with a nutty aroma. Working quickly, pour the melted butter over the egg mixture and beat well. Scatter the raspberries in the tart case. Pour the warm batter over the raspberries. Bake in the still-hot oven for about 45 minutes, until the top resembles a golden meringue. Let cool for 30 minutes before serving. Cut into slices and serve with chilled cream, if liked.

little raspberry & rose cobblers

600 g fresh raspberries, half of them frozen

for the cobbler bases

petals of 2 pink or red roses, washed and dried (optional)

50 g unsalted butter, chilled

225 g self-raising flour

a pinch of salt

50 g caster sugar (vanilla flavoured if available)

1 tablespoon rosewater extract

about 150 ml whole milk

icing sugar, to dust

thick cream, to serve

a non-stick, four-hole muffin tin

serves 4

Preheat the oven to 220°C (425°F) Gas 7.

Select the most attractive rose petals and put these to one side to use as decoration. Shred the remaining ones. Rub the butter into the flour and salt until it resembles fine breadcrumbs. Stir the sugar and shredded rose petals into this mixture.

Stir the rosewater into the milk and pour into the flour, mixing with a blunt knife to a fairly soft, sticky dough. Tip out onto a flour-dusted work surface and roll out until 1 cm thick. Cut out 4 rounds (approximately 15 cm wide) that will fill a four-cup baking tin.

Place the rounds gently in the tin and carefully push the frozen raspberries into the dough. Dust with icing sugar and bake for 10–15 minutes, until the dough is risen and golden brown. Remove from the oven.

Carefully lift each cobbler out of its tin and serve warm with the remaining fresh raspberries, a scattering of rose petals, a dusting of icing sugar and a jug of thick cream.

raspberries **179**

Raspberry jam, made from the freshest, sweetest fruit, and served on hot, buttered toast, really cannot be beaten for pure pleasure. And there is no boiling needed in this recipe so not only is it simple to make, you keep all the taste of the fruit, too. Commercially produced 'jam sugar' is perfect for this – it has added pectin that helps the preserve thicken to a soft set. Use 120 ml liquid pectin if you can't find this special jam sugar. More indulgence comes in the form of this classic French raspberry cream, although you can vary the fruit to what you have available – try it with strawberries or a mixture of summer berries.

uncooked freezer raspberry jam

750 g fresh raspberries

1 kg sugar with added pectin (sometimes known as 'jam sugar')

2 tablespoons freshly squeezed lemon juice

makes 2 x 500-g pots

Tip the raspberries into a bowl and crush a little with a potato masher. Stir in the jam sugar and lemon juice. Cover with clingfilm and heat on 'medium' in the microwave for about 5 minutes or until warmed through.

Uncover and stir gently to dissolve the sugar, then leave to stand overnight. Alternatively, heat in a saucepan until the sugar has dissolved.

The next day, pot up into freezer containers and freeze – keep one pot in the refrigerator for breakfast tomorrow. After removing from the freezer, store the jam in the refrigerator. Thaw before using.

raspberry cream

350 g raspberries, fresh or frozen and thawed plus 1 small punnet of fresh raspberries

5–6 tablespoons caster sugar, to taste

250 ml whipping cream, chilled

1 large egg white

sprigs of fresh mint, to serve

serves 4

Put the raspberries in a blender or food processor and blend until smooth, then press through a sieve to obtain a smooth purée; you should have about 200 ml. Stir in 4–5 tablespoons of the sugar. Set aside.

Put the cream in a large bowl and whisk with an electric mixer until it holds firm peaks. Set aside.

Whisk the egg white with 1 tablespoon of the sugar until it holds firm peaks. Fold the beaten egg white and raspberry purée into the cream.

Divide the mixture between 4 serving glasses, filling half-way. Set aside 4 fresh raspberries, then divide the remaining fresh ones between the glasses and top with the remaining raspberry cream.

Decorate the top of each with a fresh raspberry and a mint sprig. Chill for up to 6 hours. Serve cold.

Variation Use fromage frais in place of the whipped cream, or use half whipped cream and half fromage frais. This can also be made with strawberries or mixed berries, though you will have to adjust the sugar content. Sweeten the fruit purée gradually, tasting as you go, until it is to your liking.

There is nothing so comforting as a baked fruit dessert served with thick cream or a rich custard. A blackberry crumble is the most classic of desserts, but this impressive but simple brioche pudding is also well worth a try. The sweet and buttery brioche works well with the tangy blackberries and the dark purple juices should bleed into the pudding to create a pretty, marbled effect. Try and pick very sweet blackberries for both of these recipes, as they will be softer and juicier.

blackberry crumble

375 g blackberries
1 tablespoon caster sugar
1 teaspoon cornflour
130 g plain flour
75 g unsalted butter, cubed and chilled

60 g soft light brown sugar
double cream, to serve

a medium ovenproof dish, lightly buttered

serves 4

Preheat the oven to 180°C (350°F) Gas 4.

Put the blackberries in a bowl with the caster sugar and the cornflour and toss to mix. Tumble the berries into the buttered baking dish and set aside for 15–20 minutes.

Put the plain flour and butter in a large bowl and, using the tips of your fingers, rub the butter into the flour until the mixture resembles coarse breadcrumbs. Stir in the brown sugar.

Sprinkle the mixture evenly over the berries and bake in the preheated oven for 45–50 minutes, until the top is golden brown.

Let the crumble cool slightly before serving with dollops of cream spooned on top.

✳ tip

The floral aroma of blackberries can be enhanced by adding a small splash of Middle Eastern rosewater or orange blossom essence to the berries. Keep this in mind whenever you are serving or cooking with blackberries or any red berry.

baked brioche pudding with blackberries

4 brioche rolls or ½ 400-g brioche loaf
50 g butter, softened
3 eggs
300 g fresh blackberries
125 ml single cream
375 ml full-fat milk

75 g caster sugar
2 tablespoons raw (unrefined) sugar
vanilla ice cream, to serve (optional)

serves 6

Slice the brioche to give you 6–8 thin slices. Lightly butter the slices on one side and arrange them in the bottom of a medium baking dish, overlapping them slightly. Put half the blackberries on top. Repeat with the remaining brioche slices and blackberries. Put the cream, eggs, milk and caster sugar in a bowl or jug and beat to combine. Pour the mixture over the brioche in the baking dish. Cover with foil and let sit for 30 minutes to allow the brioche to absorb the liquid.

Preheat the oven to 180°C (350°F) Gas 4. Sprinkle the raw sugar over the top of the pudding and bake it in the preheated oven for 40–45 minutes, until the top of the pudding is golden. Serve warm with vanilla ice cream, if liked.

baked blueberry & granny smith pudding

2 tart green apples, such as Granny Smith

150 g blueberries

125 g plain flour

3 teaspoons baking powder

115 g caster sugar

250 ml buttermilk

1 egg

1 vanilla pod

100 g soft light brown sugar

single cream, to serve (optional)

serves 6

Preheat the oven to 180ºC (350ºF) Gas 4 and generously butter a medium baking dish. Peel and core the apples then thinly slice them directly into the baking dish, arranging them in the bottom of the dish with the blueberries.

Sift the flour, baking powder and caster sugar into a large bowl. Put the buttermilk and egg in a separate bowl. Split the vanilla pod in half lengthways and scrape the seeds from the pod directly into this bowl, then stir to combine. Pour the buttermilk mixture into the flour mixture and beat well to combine.

Pour the mixture over the fruit in the baking dish. Working quickly, put the brown sugar in a jug and add 250 ml boiling water. Stir until the sugar has dissolved. Carefully pour this mixture into the baking dish, pouring into a corner. Bake the pudding in the preheated oven for 45 minutes, until the surface feels dry and springs back when lightly touched. Serve warm with cream for pouring, if liked.

Sweet, mild blueberries are a delicious partner to tangy apples. Granny Smiths are a good all-round cooking apple as their flesh collapses when cooked, making them perfect for sweet puddings. Or use fresh blueberries to make this spectacular-looking cake. Bake it on the day you are going to eat it, but let it cool completely before assembling and serving.

cinnamon blueberry cake

175 g unsalted butter, softened

175 g caster sugar

4 large eggs, lightly beaten

a pinch of ground cinnamon

175 g self-raising flour, sifted

2 teaspoons baking powder

a pinch of salt

225 g blueberries

cinnamon icing

200 g cream cheese, chilled

100 g crème fraîche, chilled

50 g unsalted butter, softened and cubed

150 g icing sugar, sifted, plus a little extra for dusting

2 teaspoons ground cinnamon

two 20-cm sandwich tins, 4 cm deep, lightly buttered and base-lined with baking paper

serves 8

Preheat the oven to 180ºC (350ºF) Gas 4.

Put the butter and sugar in an electric mixer (or use a large mixing bowl and an electric whisk) and beat for 3–4 minutes, or until pale and fluffy. Gradually add the beaten eggs with the beaters still running, followed by the cinnamon, flour, baking powder and salt. Mix until all the ingredients are combined.

Divide the mixture between the prepared tins and spread it evenly with a spatula. Bake in the preheated oven for 20–25 minutes, or until lightly golden brown and risen. Leave to cool in the tins for 30 minutes. Tip the cakes out onto a wire rack and peel off the base papers. Leave to cool completely.

To make the cinnamon icing, whisk all the ingredients together to combine.

To assemble, place one cake on a cake stand or large serving plate and spread two-thirds of the cinnamon icing over the top – a spatula or table knife is the ideal tool to use here. Scatter three-quarters of the blueberries on top of the icing.

Place the other cake on the blueberries and spread the remaining icing over the top. Finish with the rest of the blueberries. Dust with a little icing sugar.

Clafoutis, a custard-like batter baked with whole cherries, is a speciality of the Limousin region. It is one of the finest French desserts and easy to make. The only drawback is that the cherry season is a short one. Plums, pears and apples work well as substitutes, but rhubarb is fantastic, almost better than the original. Rhubarb is also a classic ingredient of the fruit fool, combined here with strawberries too. These two fruits have an extraordinary affinity, which is fortunate as they come into season at the same time of year.

rhubarb clafoutis

500 g fresh rhubarb, cut into 3-cm slices

200 ml whole milk

200 ml double cream

3 eggs

150 g sugar

¼ teaspoon ground cinnamon

a pinch of salt

1 vanilla pod, split lengthways with a small sharp knife

50 g plain flour

a baking dish, about 30 cm diameter, greased with butter and sprinkled with sugar

serves 6

Bring a large saucepan of water to the boil, add the rhubarb and cook for 2 minutes, just to blanch. Drain and set aside.

Put the milk, cream, eggs, sugar, cinnamon and salt in a bowl and mix well. Using the tip of the knife, scrape the vanilla seeds into the mixture. Add the flour and whisk well.

Preheat the oven to 200°C (400°F) Gas 6.

Arrange the rhubarb in the prepared baking dish. Pour the batter over the top and bake in the preheated oven for 40–45 minutes, until puffed and golden.

rhubarb, strawberry & rose fool

400 g fresh rhubarb

3 tablespoons caster sugar

225 g fresh, ripe strawberries, plus a few extra to garnish

2–3 tablespoons rose syrup or rosewater and extra caster sugar

300 g Greek yoghurt

284-ml carton whipping cream

6 glasses or glass serving dishes

serves 6

Slice the rhubarb and put it in a saucepan with the sugar and 2 tablespoons water. Put a lid on the pan and heat over low heat until the fruit comes to the boil, then turn the heat down and simmer for 7–10 minutes until the fruit is soft. Tip the fruit into a sieve over a bowl and drain off the juice.

Hull the strawberries, put 225 g of them in a food processor and whizz until smooth. Add the drained rhubarb and 1 tablespoon rose syrup or 2 teaspoons rosewater with 1 tablespoon caster sugar and whizz again. Tip the purée into a bowl and leave to cool. Tip the yoghurt into a large bowl. In a separate bowl, whip the cream until just holding its shape and sweeten to taste with rose syrup or rosewater and sugar. Fold half the cream into the yoghurt. Fold half the puréed strawberry and rhubarb into the yoghurt and cream mixture then lightly mix the remaining cream and the rest of the rhubarb and strawberry purée to create a marbled effect.

Spoon the fool into individual glasses and chill until ready to serve. Slice the remaining strawberries and sprinkle with a few drops of rose syrup or a little sugar. Use the strawberry slices to decorate the top of each glass.

rhubarb custard & crumble tartlets

pastry

250 g plain flour

125 g unsalted butter, chilled and cubed

85 g golden caster sugar

1 egg

crumble

100 g plain flour

50 g unsalted butter, chilled and cubed

40 g golden caster sugar

rhubarb custard

360 g rhubarb, trimmed and chopped into small pieces

130 g golden caster sugar

3 eggs

a few drops of vanilla extract

130 ml double cream

a baking tray, lined with greaseproof paper

6 x 9-cm loose-based fluted tartlet tins, greased

makes 6

Creamy rhubarb custard tarts with crumbly butter biscuit on top. If you like, you can skip the crumble step and simply crush 170 g good, shop-bought shortbread instead. For an extra helping of decadence, serve with custard. If you have plenty of rhubarb, you can even make more of the mashed rhubarb, then push it through a sieve to make a lovely coulis for pouring onto the tartlet. Using forced rhubarb will make it a fantastic vibrant pink.

Preheat the oven to 180°C (350°F) Gas 4.

To make the crumble, mix the flour, butter and sugar in a food processor. Bring the dough together with your hands and transfer to a lightly floured surface. Roll with a rolling pin until about 3 mm thick, then place on the prepared baking tray. Bake in the preheated oven for 15 minutes, or until pale gold. Remove from the oven (leaving the oven on) and leave to cool completely, then crush into crumbs and set aside.

To make the pastry, put the flour, butter and sugar in a mixer until you get crumbs. Add the egg and mix again. Take the dough out of the mixer and bring together into a ball. If you prefer, you can make the dough by hand, but it's easier to do this if the butter is grated or very finely chopped.

Put the dough on a lightly floured surface and roll with a rolling pin until 3–4 mm thick. Line the tartlet tins with the pastry and trim the excess dough neatly around the edges. Blind bake for 10 minutes, or until pale gold. Leave the oven on.

To make the rhubarb custard, put the rhubarb in a roasting tray, sprinkle over the sugar and give it a stir. Cover with foil and roast in the hot oven for about 20–25 minutes, until soft. Remove from the oven, leave to cool for a few minutes, then blitz roughly in a food processor or mash with a fork.

Reduce the oven temperature to 150°C (300°F) Gas 2.

Whisk the eggs and vanilla extract together. Pour the cream into a saucepan over low heat and gently bring to the boil, stirring frequently. Remove from the heat and whisk in the eggs and vanilla and then the rhubarb until well combined.

Fill each tartlet shell up to the top with rhubarb custard and bake in the hot oven for 15–20 minutes, until the filling no longer wobbles when you shake the tartlet. Remove from the oven and scatter crumble over the top. Leave to cool slightly before serving or even better, serve chilled.

index

credits

Key: a=above, b=below, r=right,
l=left, c=centre, bg = background.

recipe credits

Ghillie Basan
Pages 18l, 31l, 55l, 59r, 63l,
66l, 79l, 86, 104l, 113r

Fiona Beckett
Pages 63r, 83l, 84l, 112, 147,
173l, 173r, 187r

Celia Brooks Brown
Pages 108l, 125br

Maxine Clark
Pages 15bl, 23br, 31r, 41r, 55r,
60l, 69, 73ar, 76l, 79r, 89bl,
108r, 125ar, 145, 155l, 160l,
160r, 179r, 180l

Ross Dobson
Pages 11r, 12r, 16, 21, 23ar,
24, 37l, 38r, 46l, 46r, 51ar, 64,
66r, 70r, 75l, 84r, 93l, 94r, 97l,
97r, 103l, 103r, 107l, 107r, 118l,
132l, 134, 139r, 144, 151l,
156r, 159r, 167l, 167r, 169,
174l, 179l, 183l, 183r, 184l,

Tonia George
Pages 15br, 20, 27l, 41l, 60r,
87r, 127r, 131r, 135r, 177al

Brian Glover
Pages 114l, 117r, 118r, 120,
121, 131l

Amanda Grant
Pages 15al, 51al, 73al, 73br,
87l, 127l, 177br

Annie Nichols
Page 12

Jane Noraika
Page 17l

Elsa Petersen-Schepelern
Page 143ar

Louise Pickford
Pages 38l, 42r, 73bl, 83r, 101br,
151r, 155r, 177ar

Isidora Popovic
Pages 28, 32l, 56, 123, 104r,
114r, 132r, 152r, 174r, 188

Sarah Randell
Pages 33, 146, 159l, 163, 164,
184r

Annie Rigg
Page 143bl

Jennie Shapter
Page 125bl

Fiona Smith
Pages 17r, 32r, 65l, 65r, 70l,
76r, 89al, 98r, 101al, 109

Sonia Stevenson
Pages 15ar, 23al, 37r, 143br

Linda Tubby
Pages 42l, 45l, 45r, 51bl, 89ar,
135l

Sunil Vijayakar
Pages 94l, 101bl, 113l

Fran Warde
Pages 125al, 177bl

Laura Washburn
Pages 11l, 18r, 23bl, 27r, 49l,
49r, 59l, 75r, 89br, 93r, 98l,
101ar, 117l, 122, 139l, 140,
141l, 141r, 143al, 148r, 180r,
187l

Lindy Wildsmith
Pages 51br, 148l, 152l, 156l,
168,

photography credits

Martin Brigdale
Pages 4, 6br, 10, 18, 19, 22al,
22bl, 30, 37, 41, 44, 45, 48ar,
48bl, 50bl, 54ar, 56b, 58, 62,
69, 78, 88ar, 88br, 93, 109,
116, 122l, 142br, 154, 163,
181, 186

Peter Cassidy
Pages front endpapers, 5bl, bcl
& br, 6bl, 15ar, 15bl, 23ar, 23bl,
24bg, 27l, 27bg, 28bg, 29, 32,
33bg, 42 both, 46bg, 49, 51ar,
51bl, 54al, 54br, 55, 56bg, 57,
60bg, 63, 66, 69bg, 73ar, 73bl,
76bg, 80, 82, 83l, 84, 86 both,
88bl, 89ar, 89bl, 98 both,
101ar, 101bl, 103, 104ar,
104bg, 105, 106al, 107, 108bg,
110, 112 a & b, 114-115 all,
119, 120, 121l&r, 122r, 123 all,
124ar, 125ar, 125bl, 127l, 130,
133, 134bg, 135bg, 136, 138,
140-141 all, 142bl, 143ar,
143bl, 144b, 145l, 145r, 146
both, 151l&r, 153, 155, 156r,
160l&r, 161, 169bg, 172, 173,
175, 176ar, 177ar, 177bl, 179,
187, 189

Nicki Dowey
Pages 16bg, 84bg

Tara Fisher
Pages 2, 6ar, 14al, 50al, 50br,
72al, 72br, 87l, 122bg, 124bl,
126, 148, 152, 156l, 168l,
176br

Jonathan Gregson
Pages 5ar, 135, 167bg, 173bg,
176al, 179bg, 183bg

Caroline Hughes
Pages 33al, 48al, 76, 94

Richard Jung
Pages back endpapers, 3, 5acl,
acr, & bcr, 8, 11r, 12bg, 13,
16al, 17bg, 20r, 21al&ar, 22ar,
25, 28, 31l, 36, 38, 39, 46a
both, 47, 48br, 50ar, 52, 59,
65bg, 68, 71, 74, 79, 90, 92,
95, 96, 97, 102, 106ar, bl, &br,
113r, 117, 118, 128, 132, 134,
139 both, 144a, 149 l & r 157,
159, 166, 167, 170, 174, 182,
183, 184l, 188, 192

Sandra Lane
Page 63bg

Lisa Linder
Pages 66bg, 142al, 155bg

William Lingwood
Pages 54bl, 75

James Merrell
Page 142ar

Diana Miller
Pages 16ar, 17a, 31r, 56a, 65,
70, 72ar, 77, 88al, 99, 100al

David Munns
Pages 100ar

Noel Murphy
Pages 14bl, 21bg, 22br, 60,
108

Peter Myers
Pages 12, 14ar, 14br

Steve Painter
Page 15al, 15br, 18bg, 23al,
23br, 51al, 51br, 73al, 73br,
89br, 89br, 101al, 101br, 125al,
125br, 143al, 143br, 177al,
177br, 190-191

© Steve Painter
Page 1

William Reavell
Pages 45bg, 120bg

Claire Richardson
Pages 24, 104al, 168r

William Shaw
Page 124br

Yuki Sugiura
Pages 20l, 26, 40, 61, 87r,
127r, 131

Debi Treloar
Pages 124al, 176bl

Pia Tryde
Page 184r

Simon Upton
Page 11l

Ian Wallace
Pages 43, 72bl, 100br

Kate Whitaker
Pages 3bg, 5bg, 7, 9, 11bg,
31bg, 32bg, 33ar, 35, 37bg,
38bg, 41bg, 49bg, 53, 59bg,
64 both, 67, 70bg, 75bg, 79bg,
81, 83bg, 85, 87bg, 91, 93bg,
94bg, 97bg, 100bl, 103bg,
107bg, 111, 112bg, 113bg,
113l, 117bg, 118bg, 121bg,
127bg, 129, 131bg, 132bg,
137, 144bg, 145bg, 147,
148bg, 149bg, 150, 151bg,
152bg, 156bg, 158, 159bg,
160bg, 162, 163bg, 164bg,
165, 168bg, 169l&r, 171,
174bg, 178, 180bg, 184bg,
185, 187bg

Polly Wreford
Pages 5al, 6al, 34, 83r, 164,
180

Francesca Yorke
Page 188bg